D0612167

Cultural China Series

Li Xianyao
Luo Zhewen

CHINA'S MUSEUMS
Treasures of Civilization

Translated by Martha Avery

CHINA
INTERCONTINENTAL
PRESS

图书在版编目（CIP）数据

中国博物馆：英文／黎先耀，罗哲文著；（美）艾梅霞译 . —2 版 .
—北京：五洲传播出版社，2010.1

ISBN 978−7−5085−1699−8

I. ①中... II. ①黎... ②罗... ③艾... III. ①博物馆−简介−中国−英文
IV. ①G269.26

中国版本图书馆 CIP 数据核字（2009）第 191280 号

CHINA'S MUSEUMS
Treasures of Civilization

Author: Li Xianyao & Luo Zhewen
Translator: Martha Avery
Executive Editor: Deng Jinhui
Art Director: Yang Jingfei
Photo Credit: Luo Zhewen, Li Xianyao, Liang Xiurong,
          Yang Jingyun et al
Publisher: China Intercontinental Press (6 Beixiaomachang, Lianhuachi
    Donglu, Haidian District, Beijing 100038, China)
Tel: 86-10-58891281
Website: www.cicc.org.cn
Printer: C&C Joint Printing Co., (Beijing) Ltd.
Format: 720 × 965mm 1/16
Edition: Jan. 2010, 2nd edition, 3rd print run
Price: RMB 99.00 (*yuan*)

Contents

Foreword
Reading the History of Chinese Civilization from Its Museums

China has an ancient civilization with a very long history and understanding it solely through the study of documents is clearly inadequate. A wealth of material has been preserved on China's vast territory as well as underground, much of which has been collected and is exhibited in various kinds of museums. This raw material of history can to a degree be thought of as more valuable for our understanding of the past than documents and historical records.

One can see many of China's cultural treasures in Western museums. Some of these are exquisite works of art, but at the same time they are fragments that have been removed from their original matrix. To enjoy a complete and systematic experience of Chinese cultural history, one must visit the museums of their native land. Although there are Dunhuang sutras in the British Museum, stolen by Aurel Stein, Dunhuang itself and the center of Dunhuang Studies remain in China. Although quite a few treasures from the Yuanmingyuan (old Summer Palace) were looted by British and French troops and are now exhibited in France at Fontainebleu, the majority of choice pieces remain in the Palace Museum in Beijing.

In the past, China's antiquities and most artworks were kept in the recesses of the residences of aristocratic families and the imperial clan. The public at large was not able to see them. China's modern museums started from the Westernization Movement of the early 20th century and the overthrow of the feudal imperial court during the Xinhai Revolution (1911). Only after this was the public allowed to enter the great halls and pavilions and enjoy the fruits of the civilization of their own ancestors. In the past thirty years, due to China's "reform and opening up" policies as well as to the development of a market economy, travel, tourism, and cultural exchange have greatly increased. China's socialist museums have developed along with these changes: they have been rebuilding and expanding, adding new buildings, increasing collections, modernizing exhibition facilities and strengthening archaeological research. There are now some 2,500 museums of all varieties in China. Visitors from both China and abroad have increased, with very positive results in the realm of education as well as in simple enjoyment.

Museums are a sort of three-dimensional encyclopedia. In the West, the Goddess of the Muse has been considered a kind of guide to Western culture. The Temple of the Muse at Atlantis was originally a comprehensive cultural arts organization and Western museums hark back to this early beginning. In China, museums originated in the collections of the ancient imperial families. They too were of a comprehensive nature and the cultural guide to the East was termed a *"bo-wu"* gentleman, or a man in command of broad or extensive matters. The term "museum" in China, *"bo-wu-guan,"* means a place devoted to broadly-conceived matters.

Many of the museums selected for this book have been designated as key protected cultural sites by China. Some have been included in the United Nations' UNESCO List of World Cultural Heritage Sites. We hope that this volume can serve as a guide to visitors in understanding these museums.

National Treasures

As an ancient country, China has given expression to tremendous creative capacity and its museums are a treasure trove of Eastern civilization. If you are able to place yourself in their midst, you will find that they delight the eye and nourish the mind.

Palace Museum

Address: Beijing, Jingshan Qian Jie, #4
Website: newweb.dpm.org.cn

I

The Palace Museum is situated in the center of Beijing, the capital city of China. It was established on October 10, 1925, and is China's largest museum.

The museum is also known as the "Purple" Forbidden City in Chinese, or the "Forbidden City" as it is commonly known in English. It covers 720,000 square meters and was the imperial palace for a succession of twenty-four emperors and their dynasties during the Ming (1368–1644) and Qing (1616–1911) periods of Chinese history. The museum is also China's largest and most complete architectural grouping of ancient halls. Construction was begun in 1420, the eighteenth year of Yongle of the Ming dynasty, so the site has existed for the past 590 years.

More than 70 halls of various sizes, containing more than 8,700 rooms, comprise the Forbidden City. These halls are aligned along a north-south axis, and extend out on either side in an east-west

The Palace Museum.

The Three Great Halls in the Forbidden City.

The recessed ceiling of the Taihe Hall in the Forbidden City.

symmetry. The central axis not only passes through the Purple Forbidden City, but extends south to Yongding Gate, and north to the Bell and Drum Towers, altogether some eight kilometers in length. This passage through the entire city of Beijing symbolizes the centrality of imperial power: the imperial seat is at the very center of this line. The architectural design lines up the buildings in neat array and with imposing scale. In a concentrated form, this assemblage expresses China's artistic traditions in the setting of China's unique architectural style.

Entering the Forbidden City from Tian'an Men (Gate), one first moves straight through the Duan Gate to arrive at Wu Men, or the great Wu Gate. The popular name for Wu Men is the Five Phoenix Tower, which marks the front entrance to the Purple Forbidden City. Going through Wu Men, spread out before one is a broad

A panorama picture of the Palace Museum taken by satellite.

courtyard with the twisting course of the Jinshui Creek (Gold Water Creek) passing from west to east like a jade belt. Five marble bridges have been constructed over this waterway. Passing through the Taihe Gate to the north of the bridges one reaches the core of the Purple Forbidden City, the famous three great halls called Taihe Hall, Zhonghe Hall, and Baohe Hall.

Taihe Hall is 26.92 meters high, or 35.05 if the platform is included, and occupies a space of around 2,377 square meters. It is the largest hall in the Palace. A red-lacquered dais around two meters high sits in its center, on which is placed a golden lacquered and carved dragon throne. Behind the throne is a screen carved with dragons. On either side of the dais are six great golden pillars with vigorous golden dragons coiling up them. In the recessed ceiling well above the throne is an extremely large coiled golden dragon, with a silvery pearl suspended from its mouth. The Taihe Hall was the location of the Emperor's most important ceremonies, such as his own inauguration, his birthday, New Years, the arrival of winter, and so on.

The marble royal ramp of the Baohe Hall in the Forbidden City.

Behind the Taihe Hall lies the Zhonghe Hall. This is a square hall with four ridge poles along the roofline that unite at the top in a large, round, gilded topknot called a *baoding*. The profile of the building is extremely beautiful. When the Emperor was about to officiate at important ceremonies, he would first rest in this building and receive visits of his various Ministers.

Behind the Zhonghe Hall is the Baohe Hall. In the Qing dynasty, every New Year's Eve, the Emperor would hold a great banquet in this hall. This also was

The bridal chamber for emperors of the Qing dynasty.

where the highest exam of the *Ke-ju* exam system was held.

Emerging from the Baohe Hall and following the stone stairs downwards one arrives at an open rectangular courtyard. This space divides the Purple Forbidden City into front and back. To the south of the square are the three main Halls and, to east and west of them are the Wenhua Hall and the Wuying Hall. These are commonly called the "Outer Court," where the Emperor primarily conducted affairs of state. To the north of the square, inside the Qianqing Gate, was the Inner Sanctum. In the Qing dynasty, this is where the Emperor and his Empresses and Concubines lived. The main buildings include the Qianqing Palace, the Jiaotai Hall, the Kunning Palace, and six palaces to east and west.

The Qianqing Palace was at one time where the Emperor slept. During the Qing dynasty, however, the emperors used this as a place of daily administrative affairs. Later emperors also met foreign emissaries here. Behind the Qianqing Palace is the Jiaotai Hall, which is where memorials to the Empress were conducted and where she received congratulations on her birthday. It also is where the Qing dynasty's twenty-five "treasures" were kept, the twenty-five seals by use of which the Emperor manifested his rule. Behind the Jiaotai Hall is the Kunning Palace, which was originally a sleeping chamber for the Empress. Later in the Qing dynasty it was made into a place where offerings to gods were made and also where the Emperor was married.

The Qianqing Palace, the Jiaotai Hall, and the Kunning Palace together constituted the Rear Three Palaces, their placement being basically the same as the Front Three Halls, but with decoration and coloring that were markedly different. The Front Three Halls used dragons as a primary motif. The Rear Three Palaces saw phoenixes gradually increase until there were numerous flying phoenixes, dancing phoenixes, phoenixes with peonies and other such decorative elements.

The East and West Six Palaces, where the concubines lived, were commonly known as the "Three Palaces and Six Courtyards." Today the Six Palaces of the East have been made into exhibition halls

The Taihe Hall in the Forbidden City.

The dragon throne in the Taihe Hall in the Forbidden City.

in order to display the rare paintings, ceramics, bronzes, and various crafts that were collected and kept in the Palace. The Six Palaces of the West are basically as they were, unchanged, so that people can see the actual living conditions of the feudal period, the reality of how royalty lived.

The most notable building is the Yangxin Hall, the "Cultivating the Mind" Hall. Qing-dynasty emperors mostly lived here from the Emperor Yongzheng onward, or for some two hundred years. The Yangxin Hall therefore became the center of daily governing activities. Emperors often received Ministers here and issued decrees and orders. Two thrones were placed in the eastern room of the Yangxin Hall, to front and back; between them was suspended a golden-colored screen. This was where the Empress Dowager Cixi ruled from behind the screen (she lived from 1835 to 1908, was of the clan of Yehenala, and she ruled from behind the screen in two periods in 1861 and 1873).

From the Yangxin Hall moving northwards, one courtyard succeeds another in quiet elegance and serenity. Among these are the

Changchun Palace and the Chuxiu Palace, the latter being where Cixi once lived. Right now, the display in the Chuxiu Palace is as Cixi had it arranged on the occasion of her fiftieth birthday.

Emerging from the Chuxiu Palace, not far to the east, is the Yuhuayuan, or Imperial Garden. The area of the Yuhuayuan is small and intimate; its architecture and atmosphere are completely different from the front parts of the Palace. The pavilions and small buildings are set in the midst of pools and pine trees, fake mountains appear to be made of grotesque stones, there are potted garden landscapes, wisteria and bamboo. In the northeast of the Palace is also the Ningshou Palace Garden, where the Emperor Qianlong (Qing dynasty Gaozong Aisin-Gioro Hongli, reigned 1736–1795) cultivated his mind after returning to power.

Coming out of the Yuhuayuan Garden and following the passageway, one arrives at the northern gate of the Purple Forbidden City called the Shenwu Men. Opposite this gate is Jingshan Hill. This small hill was built from dirt derived from digging out the moat

The Thousand Autumn Pavilion in the Imperial Garden in the Forbidden City.

in the Ming-dynasty building of the Purple Forbidden City. Standing on the top of the hill and looking out over the Palace one sees wave after wave of buildings, crest after crest of rooflines and walls.

II

The Purple Forbidden City is also a great treasury of art objects. Great collections of paintings, calligraphy, sculpture, inscriptions, bronzes, ceramics, textiles and embroideries, jewels, clocks, articles made of gold and silver, and so on are kept here. The collection contains around 1.5 million items. The Palace Museum also has preserved around nine million historical documents and materials from the Ming and Qing dynasties. These represent an important original resource for the study of the past five hundred years of China's history. Many of the more important documents can be seen in the special exhibition hall of the Palace.

Hall of Calligraphy and Painting

This is located in the Wuying Hall. An exhibition called "Palace Museum paintings through the ages" is open every year from April 15 to November 2, and exhibits famous paintings from the Jin (265–420) to Qing dynasties. Some of the more famous works held in the collection are done by Lu Ji (261–303, a Jin-dynasty scholar), Yan Liben (601–673, a Tang-dynasty Painter), Gu Hongzhong (a Five Dynasties Southern Song painter), Zhang Zeduan (a Song-dynasty painter), and Yan

The Sanxi Hall (Three Treasure Hall) in the Palace Museum that collects ancient calligraphic treasures.

Han Xizai's Evening Banquet painted by Gu Hongzhong.

Zhenqing (709–785, a Tang-dynasty calligrapher), Liu Gongquan (778–865, a Tang-dynasty calligrapher), Mi Fu (1051–1107, a Northern Song calligrapher). The work that draws the most attention is by Wang Xizhi (around 303–361, a Jin-dynasty calligrapher).

Hall of Ceramics

This is in the Wenhua Palace. The Palace Museum has around 350,000 ceramic items in its collections, among which around 400 masterpieces are on display. China is the homeland of ceramics. "Painted pottery" already existed some 6,000 years ago here; by the time of the Shang dynasty (1600–1046 BC), primitive porcelains were being fired; after another 1,000 years, actual porcelain was made during the Eastern Han period (25–220). Since the Tang dynasty (618–907), Chinese ceramics have been renowned worldwide. Their technological achievements as well as outstanding artistic qualities have had a profound influence on the ceramic production of many other countries.

Treasures Gallery

These are displayed in the eastern and western corridors of the Huangji Hall, eastern corridor, the Yangxing Hall, the Leshou

Pavilion, and the Yihexuan Hall. On display here are gold and silver, jade and exotic items collected by the Qing court. These were all used for various purposes including ceremonial, as offerings, as clothing, as ornament, and in daily life, as well as to adorn the rooms of the court.

The Clock Gallery

Fengxian Hall is where the Qing-dynasty emperors made offerings to the tablets of their ancestors; now it has been opened up and made into the Clock Gallery. These clocks were mainly collected during the Qianlong and Jiaqing periods (1736–1820) of the Qing dynasty. Some were made in Guangzhou and Suzhou, as well as the workshop within the Palace, others came from England, France, and Switzerland. Clocks made in China were mostly decorated with gold, pearls, jade, and gems. Their form reflected traditional architectural forms such as pagodas, towers, and miniature landscapes. The clocks of England, France and other countries in turn imitated Western styles and architecture.

Hall of Bronzes

This is located in the Chengqian Palace and palaces called the Zhai Palace and the Jingren Palace, and mainly exhibits bronzes from the Shang dynasty to Warring States period (475–221 BC). In the Shang and Zhou (1046–256 BC) slave society, bronzes were regarded as ceremonial objects that differentiated one's status. By the Warring States period, items appeared that were actually used by the feudal system that was in the process of forming, items such as coins, stamps or seals, tallies, measuring devices and so on. The Palace Museum has more than 15,000 bronzes in its collection that date from all periods, of which close to 1,600 pieces have inscriptions on them.

Gold and Silver Hall

This is in the Jingyang Palace's Gold and Silver Hall. It currently displays more than 100 items from the collection that all date to the Qing dynasty.

Taipei Palace Museum

Address: Taipei City, Shilin Wai, Zhishan Lu Er Duan, #221
Website: www.npm.gov.tw

    The Taipei Palace Museum is located in the northwestern part of Taipei City. Itfaces Shuangxi Park and is surrounded by verdant trees and rolling hills. The palace was constructed as a replica of the Beijing Palace Museum. It has an area of more than 10,000 square meters and is grand and imposing in character—approximately 700,000 historical items and works of art are stored here in a magnificent four-storied building. The construction of the Taipei Palace Museum was begun in 1962 and completed in the summer of 1965. Some 240,000 of the items that are kept here originally belonged to the Beijing Palace Museum.

A panorama of the Taipei Palace Museum.

The Taipei Palace Museum.

In 1949, 3,824 crates of objects were moved to Taiwan. Among these were the great treasures of "*hua-xia*," a term that refers to "China" but in a more comprehensive cultural sense. These included Shang and Zhou bronzes, jades, works of calligraphy from Jin and Tang dynasties onward, paintings from Tang and Song (960–1279) dynasties onward, ceramics from famous kilns from Song and Yuan (1206–1368) dynasties onward, bamboo items, rare books, documents from the Qing dynasty, as well as sculptures, jades, lacquer works, enamels, and so on.

Most of the items on display are shown in the main building of the museum. This building is divided into four levels, with the main entrance being on the second floor. The great hall of the second floor has a bronze bust of Sun Zhongshan (Sun Yatsen), made as a replica of the one in Nanjing at Sun Yatsen's

Mao Gong *ding* (a kind of ancient vessel, or tripod caldron).

The Sanxi Hall Tea House in the Taipei Palace Museum.

tomb. Around this sculpture hang very famous paintings and works of calligraphy; in the corridor leading to Sun Yatsen are two of the most famous "long scrolls" in the history of Chinese art.

Several national treasures are on the must-see list for visitors. Among these is the Mao Gong *ding* dating from Western Zhou, unearthed during the latter years of the Qing dynasty in the Daoguang reign (1850) in the province of Shaanxi. The height of this *ding* is 53.8 centimeters and its diameter is

The jade Chinese cabbage displayed in the Taipei Palace Museum.

47.9 centimeters. It has three legs or feet and two upright handles or ears. Its ornamentation is very simple as is the exterior. On the inside of the *ding* is an inscription of 491 characters, the longest inscription of any known Chinese bronze.

Huai Su's calligraphy displayed in the Taipei Palace Museum.

A large number of calligraphies and paintings by famous painters are exhibited in the Taipei Palace Museum. These include Li Gonglin (1049–1106, notable Song-dynasty painter), Chen Juzhong (years of birth and death unclear, a Southern-Song painter), Qiu Ying (around 1509–1551, a Ming-dynasty painter), Wang Hui (1632–1717, an early Qing-dynasty painter), Fan Kuan (around 950–1027, Song-dynasty painter), Guo Xi (1023–around 1085, Song-dynasty painter), Wang Xizhi (303–361, the Jin-dynasty calligrapher), and others.

The Taipei Palace Museum also contains a number of famous "items of the scholar's studio." Among these the most representative are the inkstones of the Song-dynasty Su Dongpo (1037–1101), the Northern Song calligrapher and literati figure, and of Zhao Mengfu (1254–1322), the famous Yuan-dynasty calligrapher.

The permanent display of the Taipei Palace Museum contains twenty thousand objects. These are rotated once every three months. Every ten years is a full cycle, so that even rare objects can be exhibited and seen by everyone.

Capital Museum

Address: Beijing City, Xicheng District, Fuxingmenwai Dajie, #16
Website: www.capitalmuseum.org.cn

The Capital Museum is a comprehensive museum displaying items relating to the cultural history of the Beijing region. Preparations for the museum began in 1953, and it was officially opened to visitors in 1981. The original museum was located on the site of a National Monument, the Beijing Temple of Confucius. The current museum is located on the western extension of Chang'an Street in a building that was opened in December of 2005 and that had its official inauguration on May 18, 2006. The new museum has exhibition space of 24,800 square meters and has a total "building area" of 63,390 square meters. It has two floors underground and five above ground. The northern part of the museum features a "green"

The Capital Museum.

square, and there is a recessed bamboo garden to the east. The building (above ground) is 152 meters from east to west and 66 meters from north to south; it is 41 meters high.

The Capital Museum is itself a work of art, melding both classical aesthetics and contemporary building features. The huge atrium continues the tradition of using deep-set eaves in Chinese architecture; the use of stone for the walls symbolizes the city walls in Chinese antiquity. Outside the door of the northern hall is a Qing-dynasty flight of steps; inside the great hall is a Ming-dynasty *pai-lou* or gate that symbolizes the "central axis" that is characteristic of Chinese architecture.

The permanent exhibition includes ten sections that exhibit 675 objects, as well as a large number of illustrations and photographs. Six primary episodes in the history of Beijing have been selected to depict the cultural changes and unique history of the city and the region. These include the ceremonies surrounding the founding of the People's Republic of China, the May Fourth Movement, the era of the Qing-dynasty emperors Kangxi, Yongzheng and Qianlong, the battle to protect Beijing, and the Dadu period of the Yuan dynasty. These narrate the special flavor of the history of the capital and express the fact that it represents an amalgamation of many

The Central Hall of the Capital Museum.

The exhibition titled "Traditional aspect of old Beijing."

cultures and peoples who have gradually formed what has become not only a national capital but a cultural center. Another exhibition focuses on the traditional aspect of old Beijing, namely the life in *hutong*s and courtyard houses. In dramatic fashion, it displays the life of an "old Beijinger," as well as a household in a *hutong* or Beijing alley. These show all the various aspects of daily life, including the focus on exquisite craftsmanship that was characteristic of the old days.

The Museum also displays a number of masterpieces in sections that include ancient ceramics, bronzes from the Yan region [where Beijing is located], ancient calligraphy, painting, jades, Buddhist arts, and treasures of the scholars' studio. These seven sections are meant to supplement and deepen the visitors' understanding of Beijing culture. A total of 5,622 articles are exhibited in this area.

The Capital Museum is at the forefront of modern, large-scale museums in the world, with its highly impressive architecture, its wealth of exhibitions, its advanced technology and attention to aesthetics. As such, it contributes to the realization that Beijing is a historic capital, a cultural center, and an international cultural capital as well.

A Ming-dynasty colored plate with figures.

Shanghai Museum

Address: Shanghai, Renmin Dadao, #201
Website: www.shanghaimuseum.net

The scope, depth and quality of its collections, and the striking architecture and use of modern technology make the Shanghai Museum one of the most famous if not the most famous museum in China. It covers an area of 39,000 square meters, with a scale that surpasses the old museum several times. The exterior of the museum utilizes the shape of an ancient bronze ding with its rather archaic flavor. The structure and materials of the entire building, however, are an accomplishment of the most modern technology.

The Shanghai Museum is mainly a museum for ancient arts. At present it is divided into ten sections. These are: ancient Chinese bronzes, sculpture, ceramics, jades, seals, calligraphy, coin and

The Shanghai Museum.

A wood carving Guanyin statue of the Song dynasty.

currency, paintings, Ming and Qing-dynasty furniture, and crafts of China's national minorities. In addition to these ten permanent exhibitions, the museum often holds small-scale exhibitions and also exhibits articles from elsewhere on a short-term basis. The Museum also exhibits its material in museums both within China and abroad.

Among the holdings of the Museum many items are superlative works of art and are unique in the entire country. These include in particular the bronzes, calligraphy, paintings, and Ming and Qing furniture.

China's Shang and Zhou-period bronzes are an important testimony to the ancient civilization of the country. When visitors enter the Ancient Bronzes Hall, the presentation and atmosphere of the rooms expresses the cultural ambiance of the bronze age. The subdued dark-green tone of the walls imparts an ancient atmosphere, the simple and elegant display cases and the lighting are carefully designed to enhance the experience. Some 400 exquisite

bronze items are displayed in a space of 1,200 square meters, perfectly reflecting the history of the development of China's ancient bronze arts.

The Calligraphy Hall includes works from many dynasties; in chronological order it displays the history of the marvelous genius of Chinese calligraphic arts. The aura of the hall is scholarly and elegant, assisted by automatic lighting in display cases that protects the art by switching on only when the visitor is viewing a work. Among these works are a number of unique world treasures.

Da Ke *ding* (a kind of ancient vessel).

The Chinese Painting Hall of the Museum similarly

has a traditional architectural style to it, combined with an atmosphere of Confucian elegance. Around 120 masterpieces are displayed in the 1,200-square-meter exhibition space. These date from the Tang dynasty to modern times but do not include contemporary works.

Furnitures of the Ming and Qing dynasties displayed in the Shanghai Museum.

The apex of Chinese furniture making occurred during the Ming and Qing dynasties. Walking into the Ming and Qing Furniture Hall is like walking back into the gardens and rooms of the Ming and Qing dynasty. In some 700 square meters of space are exhibited some 100 pieces of superlative Chinese Ming and Qing-dynasty furniture. Among these are Ming pieces that are fluid in line and harmonious in proportion. The Qing pieces have more complex ornamentation and are often made of thicker, heavier wood.

The underground part of the Shanghai Museum contains courtyard gardens that imitate authentic Chinese traditions. Although these are hidden deeply underground, their architecture and environment seem light and airy.

The stairs and the skylight of the Shanghai Museum.

Shaanxi History Museum

Address: Shaanxi Province, Xi'an City, Xiaozhai Dong Road, #91
Webpage: www.sxhm.com

The Shaanxi History Museum is situated on Xiaozhai Dong Road in Xi'an City, Shaanxi Province. It covers 65,000 square meters, with an interior space of 55,600 square meters. The newly built modern building recreates the key principles of Tang-dynasty architecture and symbolizes the great extent of Shaanxi history and its remarkable culture.

Exhibited in the main exhibition hall are 2,700 works of art, with an exhibition line that extends 2,300 meters. The exhibition space totals 11,000 square meters and is divided into an introductory hall, permanent exhibitions, special exhibitions, and temporary exhibitions, as well as a space called the National Painting Hall.

The Museum's permanent exhibition primarily displays

The exterior of the Shaanxi History Museum.

An exhibition of tomb frescoes of the Tang dynasty.

Shaanxi's ancient civilization. Representative pieces from all periods have been selected to show the development of civilization in this region. The exhibition space of this area totals 5,051.64 square meters. It includes three exhibition rooms, divided into seven parts (Pre-history, Zhou, Qin, Western Han, Wei-Jin-Northern and Southern dynasties, Sui-Tang, and Song-Yuan-Ming-Qing). The 2,000 selected objects include: painted Neolithic ceramics reflecting early people's living conditions and their pursuit of vibrant art forms, bronzes reflecting the rise of Zhou people, bronze weapons including swords, and statuary of horses and soldiers, reflecting the way in which Qin (221–206 BC) unified "all under heaven," Tang-dynasty gold and silver objects and Tang *sancai* ceramics, reflecting the most flourishing period of feudal glory. All of this is accompanied by models of archaeological sites, and drawings, and photographs. These works systematically exhibit the ancient history of Shaanxi from 150,000 years ago to the year 1840. Since several historical periods all based their capitals on Shaanxi territory, such as Zhou, Qin, Western Han (206 BC–25 AD), Sui (581–618) and Tang, the exhibits emphasize these periods and these places. This not only expresses the broad extent of culture in ancient

A cup-holding leather bag style silver kettle of the Tang dynasty with gold-plating horses unearthed in Xi'an.

A Tang-dynasty gold bowl with lotus petals carving unearthed in Xi'an.

A Tang-triple-color ceramic camel that carries a small musical band on its back with a female performer standing in the middle singing and dancing.

Shaanxi, but also displays its high level of cultural attainment.

The temporary exhibits hall, located on the east side of the museum, presents a variety of exhibitions. These have included thirty-nine actual Tang-tomb wall paintings, including scenes that depict hunting and playing polo. Shaanxi's wall murals of this kind rank first in the country. They are fluid in concept and line, they have marvelous details, and they both depict Tang customs and are superb works of art.

The special exhibition hall is located on the west side of the museum. Its first two exhibitions were a Shaanxi bronzes exhibit (260 were on display) and a Shaanxi-through-the-dynasties terracotta masterpieces exhibit (341 objects were exhibited). The area of this hall is around 2,600 square meters.

The Shaanxi History Museum contains 370,000 objects in its collections. The more representative of these include bronzes, Tang-dynasty tomb wall paintings, terracotta statuary, ceramics (pottery and porcelain), construction materials through the dynasties, Han and Tang bronze mirrors, and coins and currency, calligraphy, rubbings, scrolls, woven articles, bone articles, wooden and lacquer and iron and stone objects, seals, as well as some contemporary cultural items and ethnic objects.

A bronze ox *zun* (a kind of ancient wine vessel) of the Western Zhou Dynasty unearthed in Qishan County, Shaanxi Province.

Henan Museum

Address: Henan Province, Zhengzhou City, Nongye Road, #8
Webpage: www.chnmus.net

The Henan Museum is one of China's oldest museums. It is a "key" museum, with modern displays and exhibitions, modernized equipment, and a unique architecture. In 1961, along with the move of the provincial capital to Zhengzhou, it moved to its current location in that city. In 1991, the museum was remodeled and in 1999 the official reopening was held, when the name was officially changed to the Henan Museum.

The new Henan Museum is set in the central section of Nongye Road in Zhengzhou City, Henan Province. It covers an area of more than 100,000 square meters, with a building area of 78,000 square meters. The exhibition hall space is more than 10,000 square meters. The building uses a combination of both traditional architecture and path-breaking new technology.

Henan is situated in the middle reaches of the Yellow River. Its ancient name is Zhongzhou, or "central region." It is one of the key regions in the rise of civilization of the progenitors of Chinese

The facade of the Henan Museum.

A Warring States period gold-plating silver belt hook inlaid with jade unearthed in Huixian County, Henan Province.

A rose-purple Chinese flowering crabapple style ceramic flower pot unearthed in Yuxian County, Henan Province.

people. Because of this, exhibitions in this museum are mostly related to the ancient history and culture of the Henan region, including objects, historical "traces," ancient architecture, archaeological discoveries, and arts and crafts. The four floors of the main building of the museum exhibit ancient Henan culture, key features of central plains culture, ancient Henan architecture, bronzes of the state of Chu, ancient Henan jade objects, and arts of the Ming and Qing dynasties. There is also a commemorative exhibition about the seventy years of the museum itself. Among objects on display are bronzes dating from the Shang, Zhou, Spring and Autumn period (770–476 BC), and Warring States period. Ceramics include earliest pieces from the Shang dynasty, to

The representative display in the main hall of the Henan Museum.

Tang-dynasty *sancai*, to Han dynasty (206 BC–220 AD) architectural models (used as funerary objects). Lacquer wares, dinosaur eggs, and other interesting items are on display as well.

In the past several decades, the collecting, protection, research, and exhibition of this museum's artifacts have seen great advances, as well as the development of educational material on these objects. Objects from the Museum's collections have traveled to America, Japan, England, Germany, France, Australia, and Denmark for exhibition and have been widely praised. The Henan Museum applies modern management systems, one of which is that its security systems of surveillance and alarms are consolidated into a central unit to ensure the safety of the objects. The automatic management system of the buildings can monitor and adjust all of the surveillance and condition systems of the various buildings. This enables ambient environmental conditions to be monitored and adjusted, to protect the collections and exhibited objects and to control the required levels of temperature and humidity.

An article for the dead of Han dynasty displayed in the Henan Museum (architectural model).

Nanjing Museum

Address: Jiangsu Province, Nanjing City, Zhongshan East Road, #321
Webpage: www.njmuseum.com

The Nanjing Museum is located inside the Zhongshan Gate of Nanjing City. Its predecessor was known as the Central Museum Preparatory Location. The complex of buildings covers 70,000 square meters and represents an amalgamation of east and west, with the great hall copying the style of a Liao-dynasty (907–1125) palace.

The Museum currently holds some 400,000 objects in its collections, among which are some of the most famous objects in China. These include the only complete set of "jade suits sewed with silver thread" in China, which are world renowned. In 1982, a

The facade of the main building of the Nanjing Museum.

Warring States period Chu State tomb was excavated, from which stellar pieces were retrieved that also form some of the extraordinary treasures in this museum.

The calligraphy and paintings collections are also very special. Among the 100,000 objects that have officially entered the collections, most are Ming- and Qing-dynasty works of artists who lived in the Jiangsu area. Among these, the most special are the "Wu Men painting school," "Yangzhou painting school," "Jinling painting school," as well as a small number of Song and Yuan-dynasty works. Most of the representative works of the modern Chinese painter Fu Baoshi (1904–1965, painter, art historian), and Chen Zhifo (1896–1962, painter modern arts educator) are stored here.

The Nanjing Museum holds the objects excavated by archaeologists in the early part of the twentieth century that were moved to Nanjing when the Palace Museum moved southward. These include excavations in Heilongjiang, Xinjiang, Yunnan, Sichuan, Gansu and other places. Collections also include artifacts from the southwest parts of China of the Naxi tribe, the Yi tribe, the Miao

The outdoor courtyard layout of the Nanjing Museum.

A south-of-Yangtze family's living room displayed in the Nanjing Museum.

tribe, and other national minorities. The museum also holds a wealth of historic documents, including memorials to the emperor of nineteenth-century figures including Weng Tonghe (1830–1904), a notable Reformist. Other documents include title deeds for land, for housing, documents for leasing fields, and tenant farmer contracts.

The Museum employs modern scientific methods of conservation, and is active in displaying its holdings, having mounted some 236 exhibitions.

An Eastern Han dynasty copper ox lamp inlaid with silver.

A Warring States period copper kettle inlaid with gold beasts.

Museum of Liaoning Province

Address: Liaoning Province, Shenyang City, Shifu Road, #363
Website: www.lnwh.gov.cn/bwg1/bwgjj.htm

The Museum of Liaoning Province was established in 1949 on Shiwei Road in the Heping District of Shenyang City. The new museum opened to the public in November of 2004, and is located on the east side of the central square that holds the Shenyang Municipal Government. The new museum has twelve exhibitions halls with a total of 8,530 square meters of exhibition space, while the building itself is 28,900 square meters in area. It is a large-scale, multi-functional, highly impressive establishment.

The exterior of the Museum of Liaoning Province.

A Western Zhou dynasty bronze utensil —a *lei* (a kind of ancient wine vessel) with a lid and coiling dragons pattern.

Historical artifacts and ancient arts are the main focus of the Museum's collections. These are divided into seventeen different categories that include paintings and calligraphy, bronzes, ceramics, lacquer ware, carvings, oracle bones, celadons, costumes, archaeological material, coins and currency, stelaes, ethnic minority artifacts, and assorted other items. Among these, some were excavated and others were "passed down through the ages," that is, inherited, not recovered from the earth. The collections occupy an important position among museum collections in China.

Painting and calligraphy collections include

"Lady of State Guo Spring outing" by the Tang Painter Zhang Xuan.

Liao ceramics collected by the Liaoning Museum.

a painting by Zhou Fang (Tang painter, dates unclear), a calligraphy work by Ouyang Xun (Tang calligrapher, 577–641), as well as Northern Song (960–1127) masterpieces. Woodblock-print editions include the Ming-dynasty Album of the Ten-bamboo Studio, the first colored woodblock print in Chinese woodblock-print history. In addition, twenty masterpieces, national treasures, from the collection of the last emperor of China are on display. These were brought out of the Purple Forbidden City by the last emperor (Pu Yi, 1906–1967) when he moved to northeastern China and were then scattered among a number of places before being assembled at the Liaoning Museum.

The ceramics collections in the museum are also quite famous and valuable. Liao porcelain is unique in the art form for its treatment of colored glazes, but the collection also includes Liao monochromes such as the lovely Liao white porcelain. Many of the ceramic forms embody nomadic characteristics, and the glazes and colors are imbued with local character. Production methods continue the traditions of the Tang and Five-dynasties kilns. Around

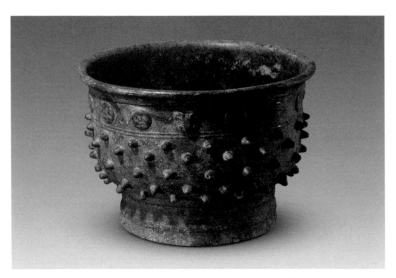

A copper *gui* called "yufu *gui*," a kind of food vessel used in the Western Zhou dynasty unearthed in Kazuo, Liaoning.

200 Liao-ceramic masterpieces are currently on display.

The Museum also presents a five-part exhibition that does an outstanding job of expressing the historical development of the Liaoning region itself. The name of the exhibition itself is "Liaohe River civilization," and its five sections include: Dawn of Civilization, Northern lands of the Shang and Zhou, Unifying "*Hua-xia*," the Qidan (Khitan) dynasty, and the Rise of the Manchu tribe.

Other permanent collections on display in the museum include an exhibition of stone inscriptions. In chronological order, this shows around 120 inscriptions dating from Eastern Han to the Ming and Qing dynasties. Among these pieces, Eastern Han, Northern Wei (386–534), and Liao imperial creations are considered national treasures. Secondly, they include ceramics from the Qing-dynasty palace. Objects include imperial *guan-yao* in particular, but also a variety of different glazes and techniques. Thirdly, they include Ming and Qing-dynasty objects made from jade, lacquer, enamel, wood, bamboo, and ivory.

Three Gorges Museum

Address: Chongqing City, Yuzhong District, Renmin Road, #236
Website: www.3gmuseum.cn

The Three Gorges Museum is located to the west of the Great People's Hall in the city of Chongqing. In between the Great Hall and the Museum is the 40,000-square-meter People's Square. The Museum occupies 30,000 square meters of land. It was opened in 2005 and the building measures 42,500 square meters in area. The predecessor to this museum was the Chongqing Museum and at present that function is preserved within the new museum as well. The objects collected by the Chongqing Museum over one-half century of amassing 170,000 treasures, as well as the large amount of cultural material that has come from the Three Gorges, can finally be properly exhibited in the new museum. The Three Gorges Museum can be considered a "comprehensive museum" that combines both history and fine arts. More than 10,000 objects are generally on display.

Entering the Three Gorges Museum, not only can you enjoy exhibitions that reflect the history, culture and spirit of the magnifi-

The Three Gorges Museum.

Part of "The magnificent Three Gorges," a panorama.

"The Great Bombing of Chongqing."

cent Three Gorges, namely, the "ancient Ba-Shu" sources of the regional culture, the changes in the twentieth century that gave rise to modern urban culture, and the experience of the War of Resistance against Japan, but one can also enjoy six exhibitions that relate to more traditional Chinese culture. These include chronological displays of paintings, ceramics, coins, and carvings, articles donated by Li Chuli, and cultural traditions of the ethnic minorities of the southwest. In addition, the visitor can experience movies that give a 360-degree full-view presentation of what the Three Gorges was like before construction of the dam began, including its environment and human geography. The visitor can revisit the scene of Chongqing during the War of Resistance against Japan, when Chongqing was the capital and suffered from bombing over a number of years. This exhibition is entitled "The Great Bombing of Chongqing," and it elicits from viewers the heartfelt desire for peace. Taken together, these exhibitions form the main subject matter of the displays at the Three Gorges Museum.

The material for the walls and the glass-sheathed exterior of the Three Gorges Museum form a relationship that mimics the Great Dam and water, and Mountains and water. The glass dome of the ceiling and the glass-sheathed walls form a union of sun and moon; the glass dome resembles a huge magnifying glass, reminding us to pass on the inheritance we have received from our forebears to the next generation, to use our "culture," which is to say all we have learned, to nurture the earth. This is precisely the mission of this museum.

Inscriptions on the White Crane Rock, Fuling, Chongqing.
White Crane Rock, located in the center of the Yangtze River in Fuling City of Chongqing, is a magnificent stone reef that extends 1,600 meters. Only a portion shows through above the surface of the water in the dry-water season in between winter and spring. Because of this, Three Gorges inhabitants from ancient times used this place as an indicator of water-level changes, and as a way to foretell the next year's harvests. Many inscriptions are carved into the rock, including 165 stanzas and more than 30,000 characters, plus eighteen illustrations of fish. The data carved on this rock gives information on 72 drought years in the more than 1,200 years from the Tang dynasty to today. The site has been called the world's most ancient hydrological station. Once the Three Gorges dam was put into effect, this White Crane Rock was submerged under forty meters of water. On May 18, 2009, the underground museum at Fuling White Crane Rock was officially opened. This is the world's only underwater museum and the "no-pressure container" that serves as a shell for the rock is the first invented in the world as a way to preserve this cultural inheritance. Visitors can ride an automatic escalator down a 90-meter incline to enter the part of the museum that is under water. They can observe the carvings on the original White Crane Rock through an observation window.

Contributions of China's National Minorities

China includes people of many nationalities. The special characteristics of each of these ethnic groups have contributed to the tapestry that constitutes Chinese civilization. The following sections describe some of the museums located around China that display their contributions.

Cultural Palace of Nationalities

Address: Beijing, Xicheng District, Fuxingmennei Dajie, #49
Webpage: www.cpon.cn

The Cultural Palace of Nationalities is located on West Chang'an Street in Beijing. It serves as a focal point where all the nationalities of the country can come together for cultural exchange: it is a microcosm of the greater family of diverse peoples that make up China. The building occupies some 32,000 square meters and is a multistoried tower-like structure. It stands 13 stories high and has two wings that flank the central hall. The roof is tiled with peacock-blue tiles that form a striking contrast to the white walls. The museum encompasses various parts including museum, exhibition halls, library, and performance hall. On October 17, 2009, the Cultural Palace of Nationalities celebrated its fiftieth anniversary with a major celebration.

Some 50,000 objects constitute the collections of the Cultural Palace of Nationalities, including scripts, costumes, and handicrafts that relate to minority people. The territory from which they are drawn extends to Tibet, Xinjiang, Inner Mongolia, Guangxi, Ningxia, Yunnan and Guizhou. The material encompasses artifacts from all 56 of modern China's ethnic minorities. It also includes historical objects from peoples who once lived on the same territories including Xiongnu (Hun), Dangxiang (Tangut), Qidan (Khitan), and Dian peoples, among

The exterior of the Cultural Palace of Minorities in Beijing.

A corner of minorities' cultural exhibition hall in Cultural Palace of Minorities in Beijing.

Minorities' garments displayed in the Cultural Palace of Minorities in Beijing.

others. Traditional clothes are a particularly striking part of the collection. There is also a wealth of religious artifacts relating to every kind of religion in China. Among the objects from Tibet are scriptures, documents, laws, treaties and books that constitute an invaluable historical record.

Historical relics are also held in this museum. They include musical instruments dating to the Tang dynasty, armor from the Yuan dynasty, items from the Western Xia (1038–1227), weapons from the Qing dynasty.

Based on these collections, the Museum has held exhibitions of ancient scripts, costumes, bronze drums, and a great diversity of other topics. As an example, an exhibition of the Dong minority of Guizhou showed local architecture using not only actual objects but models of architectural sites. It brought in young Dong boys and girls to dance, play instruments, and perform so that the audience could feel they were situated in the deep mountain passes of the Dong people.

An extensive library of books in twenty-four different national languages is located in the basement of the Museum. The languages include Han, Mongolian, Tibetan, Korean, Uighur, Kazakh, and others, in some 600,000 volumes. Among these are rarely seen scripts, and artistic works of great value in the form of golden sutras, carved woodblocks, manuscripts, paintings and early rubbings. These have scientific as well as artistic value, in narrating the history of the cultures of all of China's people.

Shenyang Palace Museum

Address: Liaoning Province, Shenyang City, Shenyang Road, #171

The Shenyang Palace Museum is located at Jing-zi Dajie in the center of the "old city" part of Shenyang City, Liaoning Province. It covers more than 60,000 square meters and is a history museum with collections and exhibits that deal mainly with Qing-dynasty art and artifacts.

Formerly called the Fengtian Palace Museum, then the National Shenyang Museum, in 1954 it was officially renamed the Shenyang Palace Museum. In 1961, the State Council placed it among the ranks of National Key Cultural Relics Protected Units. The permanent exhibits of the museum are divided into two parts, one showing historical artifacts of the court and the other showing Qing-dynasty arts and crafts.

The Shenyang Palace Museum is the only well preserved group of ancient palace buildings in the country except for the Beijing

A panorama of the East Way of the Shenyang Palace Museum displaying Manchu tent-style architectural features.

The Dazheng Hall in the Shenyang Palace Museum.

The Wensu Hall in the Shenyang Palace Museum.

The Phoenix Tower in the Shenyang Palace Museum.

Palace Museum. The complex is divided into three parts, the Eastern Way, the Central Way, and the Western Way. The architecture of the main building of the Eastern Way is characteristic of a horse-riding arrow-shooting people who used tent palaces; this Dazheng Hall once hosted tremendous ceremonies.

The main building of the Central Way was where the emperor held daily meetings with his court to conduct governmental affairs and receive ministers. Inside, objects are arranged as they were during the Qianlong period. Inside a separate hall to the west are objects used by the emperors Qianlong and Jiaqing as these two emperors made their long investigative trips

The interior of Chongzheng Hall in the Shenyang Palace Museum

The main gate of the Shenyang Palace Museum.

through the country.

On the western side of the Shenyang Palace Museum are riding grounds where horses were kept and trained, also a pavilion in which the emperor watched plays when he did his "eastern sojourn." There is also a reconstruction of a Ming-dynasty pavilion from Ningbo, which is one of the seven halls in the Qing dynasty to receive a copy of the famous Yongle-period encyclopedia known as the *Siku Quanshu*, or the Four Warehouses of All Knowledge.

Most of the Shenyang Palace Museum collections of documents and artifacts date from the Qing dynasty, though some are from the Ming. Many are of interest for their historical value but some are of great artistic value as well, such as paintings by Dong Qichang (1555–1636), a famous Ming-dynasty painter and calligrapher. Some of the more representative treasures that have been exhibited from the collections of the Museum are Qing-dynasty weapons, musical instruments, palace accouterments, ceramics, carvings, textiles and embroideries, lacquer ware, and amber.

The original throne display in the Dazheng Hall.

Inner Mongolia Museum

Address: Inner Mongolia Autonomous Region, Hohhot City, Xinhua Dongjie

This museum was formerly called the Inner Mongolia Autonomous Region Museum. It was founded on the occasion of the tenth anniversary of the establishment of the Inner Mongolia Autonomous Region, in 1957. The old museum was located at the intersection of Xinhua Dajie and Zhongshan Lu in the heart of Hohhot City, the capital of the autonomous region. The museum is now located outside the intersection of the Airport Road and the East Second Ring Road in Hohhot City. The architecture is very contemporary and impressive, while a massive *"ding"* or bronze tripod stands in front of it as a symbol of the solidarity of all nationalities.

The Inner Mongolia Museum holds more than 100,000 objects or sets of objects in its collections. Among these quite a few are rare treasures seldom seen in China, especially the artifacts relating to the northern tribes called Xiongnu (Hun), Xianbei, Qidan (Khitan),

The exterior of the Inner Mongolia Museum.

The fossil skeleton of a mammoth displayed in the Inner Mongolia Museum.

Mongolians and others. There are also a large number of cultural relics relating to northern people's customs. The Inner Mongolia Museum is a regional-level museum. One of the important sources of its collections are precious materials excavated from the earth as a result of archaeological research. These materials are one of the great attractions of the museum.

This museum has also been active in collecting and preserving contemporary items that relate to the rich local culture and local customs. At present, there are more than 3,000 sets of such objects, which reflect the lifestyles and customs of a wide variety of Mongolian and other ethnic groups in the region. Among these, notable attractions include the costumes of Mongolian women from different parts of Inner Mongolia as well as Mongolian religious artifacts.

Inner Mongolia is also known as the "Land of Fossils." Specimens shown in the Inner Mongolia Museum include massive dinosaurs, mastodons, and many other kinds of fossilized remains from the Mesozoic period that have attracted global attention.

An eagle-shaped gold crown of the Warring States period.

Xinjiang Uighur Autonomous Region Museum

Address: Xinjiang Uighur Autonomous Region, Urumqi, Xibei Road, #132

The Xinjiang Uighur Autonomous Region Museum was established in the spring of 1953 in the People's Park in Urumqi City. The new Xinjiang Uighur Autonomous Region Museum was opened with great ceremony on September 20, 2005. It is situated on Northwest Road (Xibei Road) of Urumqi City. It covers a square area of 17,288 square meters, with one floor underground and two above ground. The main building is 18.5 meters high with a glass dome that reaches 29.5 meters. The plane of the building basically forms the shape of the character "one" in Chinese. The architecture retains a strong "western-regions" flavor as well as Xinjiang regional characteristics.

The Silk Road derived its fame, of course, from silk. The Xinjiang Uighur Autonomous Region Museum has also become famous for its rich collections of silk artifacts from many periods of history. Brocades from Eastern Han are highlighted, as well as Eastern Jin (317–420), and all kinds of specialized silk-woven items from the height of the Tang. These are as lustrous and beautiful today as when they were new and display weaving techniques that were highly re-

The exterior of the Xinjiang Uighur Autonomous Region Museum.

The "Hu King" brocade unearthed from Astana ancient tombs in Turpan.

A Loulan female corpse of more than 4,000 years ago unearthed in the Silk Road.

fined many hundreds and even thousands of years ago. These are regarded as unique treasures by textile authorities and art historians around the world. A number of the articles on display here are the earliest extant examples of certain weaving technologies in China.

The Xinjiang Autonomous Region has long been a crossroads for many different kinds of people. Their diversity of scripts and cultures is exhibited in this museum through archaeological material, including documents in some twelve different scripts with a particularly large number from the Han-dynasty finds at Turpan. The documents cover military, economic, cultural, and political affairs. Clay or terracotta sculptures are also featured in the Xinjiang Museum. Among these are single-humped Central Asian camels, fat and vigorous Yuan-dynasty horses, women figurines in all postures, impressively fierce soldiers, and so on. These were sculpted in a most natural and vigorous way and have been preserved as a result of Xinjiang's arid climate.

The Xinjiang Museum has several dozen original Tang-dynasty paintings. Although these are not from the hands of famous painters, they still exhibit the vital Tang spirit. They include such subjects as women playing *weiqi* or Chinese chess, children frolicking, "eight steeds," people dancing and so on.

Other items in the collections include microliths, silver works of art, stone stelaes, coins and currency, ceramics, wooden articles. Of particular note are various foods from the Tang dynasty which, through the arid conditions, have been preserved over the passage of more than one thousand years.

In a similar vein, certain dessicated human corpses, called mummies although they were not treated with chemicals, are kept in the Xinjiang Museum. Some of these date back to 4,000 years ago. They are the earliest known such examples in China and are important in the study not only of humankind but of ethnic composition in this region at the time. Also in the museum are an Eastern-Han couple, buried together and well preserved, and a corpse from the Tang dynasty with well preserved skin and hair.

Exhibits that are currently open to the public include two from the permanent collections and two that are mid-sized displays. The first two are, "Recalling the glories of the western regions—exhibition of Xinjiang historical artifacts," and "Xinjiang Nationalities' Customs Exhibition." The second two are "Exhibition of ancient Xinjiang mummies," and "Exhibition of Xinjiang Revolutionary material."

The history exhibit shows the history of Xinjiang by using material from its rich collections and highlighting material from recent archaeological discoveries. The Customs exhibition introduces the customs and cultural lifestyles of twelve different ethnic groups in Xinjiang, including the Uighur, Kazakh, Mongolian, Kirgiz, Hui, Tajik, Uzbek, Russian, Tatar, Daur, Xibe, and Manchu.

A corner of the Uighur courtyard and house displayed in the Xinjiang People's Customs Exhibition Hall.

Tibet Museum

Address: Tibet Autonomous Region, Lhasa City, Southeast corner of
Norbulingka
Website: www.tibetinfor.com/tibetzt/xzbwg

The Tibet Museum was officially inaugurated in October of 1999, with a permanent collection that celebrates the History of Tibetan Culture. The design of the exhibit uses traditional Tibetan architecture such as Tibetan doors, beam-decoration, patterns and so on, in order to create the atmosphere of authentic Tibetan art.

The exterior of the Tibet Museum.

The History of Tibetan Culture Exhibition incorporates superb examples of several thousand years of Tibetan history, politics, religion, cultural arts, and customs. It "takes Tibetan history as the main thread and Tibetan culture as the center" in exhibiting the long history of the Tibetan people and their vast and deep culture. At the same time, most of the historical objects also express the fact that Tibet is an inalienable part of Chinese territory.

This exhibit displays around 1,000 precious objects, in a space totaling around 3,000 square meters and with an exhibition line of around 600 meters. The contents are divided into pre-history culture, indivisible history, culture and arts, and people's customs.

The seal of Yuan emperor's teacher displayed in the Tibet Museum.

Prehistory

This covers a period that stretches back fifty thousand years to three thousand years before the present. The Kano (kha-rub) and Qugong (chu-gong) sites are representative of the Neolithic in Tibet. With a large number of characteristic stone tools, pottery, bone objects and metal objects, this exhibition expresses the life of the ancient people of the Tibetan plateau. It also shows the cultural origins of the precursors of the Tibetan people, and their connections with the central plains civilization and Indus River civilization.

Indivisible History

This section includes material on different dynastic periods of Tibetan history, including Tibetan regional powers. Its main section revolves around the relationship between the Chinese central government and the Tibetan regional powers and discusses friendly relations between Han and Zang or Tibetan people. A large number of historically valuable objects are displayed as well as cultural relics that have political significance. These include seals, books, official documents, and so on, that clearly indicate the cordial relations that Han and Tibetan people have long enjoyed and the bonds of friendship due to the effective governance of Tibet by successive dynasties in China. It proves that Tibet has been an inalienable part of China since the Yuan dynasty.

Cultural Arts

This is divided into eight segments that include the development

An embroidered thanka displayed in the Tibet Museum.

of Tibetan-script books, documents and scrolls, the arts of Tibetan theater, Tibetan musical instruments, Tibetan medicine, Tibetan astronomy and calendar reckoning, Tibetan sculpture, and thanka or painting arts. Altogether, these depict an artistic and cultural overview of the last thousand years of Tibetan arts and thoroughly display the once-glorious heights of Tibetan arts and culture. The exhibited artifacts are treasures of the Tibetan Autonomous Region Cultural Relics Protection Organization that was set up after the establishment of the PRC. Some of these treasures are unique and being shown to the world for the first time; they are historical evidence of the history of Tibetan civilization.

People's Culture

This part of the exhibition is divided into six segments that include displays of Tibetan people's costumes, items of daily life, arts and handicrafts, means of communication and so on. From a variety of perspectives, these show how Tibetan people dressed, what they ate, how they lived, their marriage and funeral customs, and so on. The exhibits also reflect the friendly relations of Tibetan people with those on their borders, including the influence of Han culture on Tibetan culture and the mutual influence and interpenetration of these two traditions.

Guangxi Zhuang Autonomous Region Museum

Address: Guangxi Zhuang Autonomous Region, Nanning City, Minzu
        Dadao, #34
Website: www.gxmuseum.com

The Guangxi Zhuang Autonomous Region Museum is situated on the east side of the People's Square in Nanning City, and covers an area of 32,757 square meters. Its main exhibition building is a modern structure with southern architectural characteristics, which contains six exhibition halls. The Museum collections include more than 50,000 objects.

The "Guangxi Historical Artifacts Exhibition" exhibits all periods of Guangxi history from Primitive Society up to the Opium

The exterior of the main exhibition building of the Guangxi Zhuang Autonomous Region Museum.

War (1840–1842), reflecting local culture and the interchange with the Central Plains and neighboring regions and the process of cultural melding and development. The exhibition of the "Liujiang Man" shows the earliest hominid fossil found to date within the borders of Guangxi. It belongs to the late period of hominids and is the earliest representative of modern man found to date not only inside China but in the Southeast Asia region.

Copper phoenix lamps of the Han dynasty unearthed in Hepu, Guangxi. The necks can be turned or taken apart in order to adjust light and clean the ashes in lamp bodies. The lamp body can hold candle smoke or ashes to avoid pollution.

Stone tools manufactured in more than one hundred sites have been found in Guangxi. Mesolithic-period polished-blade stone tools and stones with finely wrought holes in them are displayed in the museum, as well as a wealth of artifacts from the Neolithic period. Neolithic sites are divided into three main types, those in caves, on hills, and on mountain slopes and artifacts are exhibited from all three. Of particular note is a large ceremonial shovel-shaped object that is 66.4 cm in length

"The ancient bronze drums Exhibit" displayed in the Guangxi Zhuang Autonomous Region Museum.

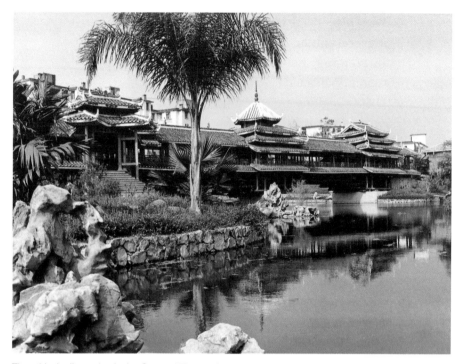

The ethical relic garden in the Guangxi Zhuang Autonomous Region Museum.

and 44.8 cm wide. The quality of its manufacture, its size, and its polishing make it a superlative work.

In the Shang and Zhou periods, two tribes who lived in Guangxi began to have political, economic and cultural relations with the Central Plains region. Certain bronze items are evidence of this cultural interchange although there is also evidence that, 2,500 years ago, during the late Western Zhou period, Guangxi's ancient inhabitants were creating their own brilliant bronze culture. Items in the Museum that demonstrate this culture include spears, axes, ladles, bells, and many other items found the "Matou Yuanlongpo" grave in Wuming County. Early inhabitants also achieved a high level of ceramic technology, with firing temperatures of 1150 degrees centigrade. Many such ceramics are on display in the Museum.

Among the bronzes exhibited are some that allow the visitor to understand something of the ancient Guangxi bronze-drum culture. There are more than 300 drums from this culture in the Museum. One such drum is exhibited in a prominent position; other bronzes include a snake-headed frog-patterned vessel called a *zun*, and other items that clearly show the influence of local artistic traditions. A group of iron objects excavated from the Northern Guangxi region indicate that Guangxi had entered the iron-culture stage by the Warring States period. Qin-dynasty evidence in Guangxi attests to a more than two-thousand-year-old practice of systematic canal-making in the region. Han-dynasty objects are primarily excavated from Han-period tombs and indicate that from this time onward the parallel cultures began to merge.

The regional-culture treasures that are exhibited include bronze drums with carved inscriptions, lacquer painted bronze basins, bronze horses, bronze phoenix lanterns, lacquer eared cups, bamboo flutes, celadon bowls, glass cups and so on. A "Yellow Dragon"

The exhibition hall of Guangxi ethical customs in the Guangxi Zhuang Autonomous Region Museum.

bronze mirror is unique among all
Three Kingdoms (220–280) bronze
mirrors. An excavated inscribed
tablet excavated from a Jin-dynasty
grave notes that "disasters are
reigning throughout the land but
south of the river all is peaceful."
This reflects the warring conditions
on the central plains during the end
of the Western-Jin period (265–
317), whereas Guangxi was relatively peaceful and the economy
was developing rapidly.

A jade cup of the Western Han dynasty.

The "Ancient Bronze Drums Ex-
hibit" displays representative works of the eight main types of
bronze drums from the Spring and Autumn period to the Qing
dynasty, together with relevant documents, drawings and models.
It narrates the chronological development, distribution, types, uses,
and modern usage of bronze drums in the region. One drum of
note is the so-called thundercloud-patterned drum, excavated from
Beiliu County in Guangxi. It has a diameter of 165 centimeters and
weighs 300 kilometers, and to date is the largest bronze drum to
have been found.

Another exhibition reflects the customs of the eleven national
minorities in Guangxi. It exhibits their costumes, weavings, dying
techniques, embroidery and so on, as well as items to do with local
festivals. The Ethnic Minorities Cultural Relics Garden is an outdoor exhibition of rooms of national minority customs. This repro-
duces certain minority-people's architecture, such as the wooden
railing buildings of the Zhuang, bamboo structure of Yao, hanging
buildings of Miao, homes of Maonan, drum towers, wind and rain
bridges of Dong, and other special features of local architectural
design.

Ningxia Museum

Address: Ningxia Hui Autonomous Region, Yinchuan City, Beijing Zhong
        Road

The Ningxia Museum was formerly the Ningxia Hui Autonomous Region Museum. Its former location was inside the Chengtian Temple in the old city district. On August 28, 2008, the new buildings of the Ningxia Museum were formally opened to the public. The new Museum is located to the east side of the People's Square in Ningxia City. It covers more than 30,000 square meters of space and is a modern museum that combines the functions of collecting, exhibiting, research, and development. There are a total of eight exhibition halls in the new museum, and the focus is on Hui nationality items (Moslem), on Western Xia items, and on petroglyphs

The exterior of the Ningxia Museum.

from the Helan Mountains.

Ningxia Historical Artifacts Exhibition

This focuses on articles from local history, from ancient times up to Ming and Qing. It is divided into sections as follows: primitive society, Shang and Zhou, Qin and Han, Sui and Tang, Song and Yuan, Ming and Qing, and mostly displays items that have been passed down through generations. Objects of natural-history interest include fossilized paleontological material. Early archaeological material includes ceramics of the Majiayao culture, and artifacts from all the dynastic periods of China that represent border-region cultures. From ancient times, the Ningxia region has been a confluence of cultures, a place where many different nationalities and peoples came together. It displays in particular the interaction of people from border regions and people of the central plains. The Ningxia historical exhibitions provide tangible evidence of this rich history.

The Western Xia (Xi Xia) History Exhibition

This exhibition portrays the historical development of the Xi Xia Kingdom (1038–1227), using excavated Western Xia artifacts com-

Display of houses of Hui nationality in the Ningxia Museum.

bined with historical documents. Yinchuan City was the Tangut Kingdom's capital. Western Xia kings, concubines, and aristocracy are buried in the tomb precinct in the eastern ranges of the Helan Mountains. Among the items on display here are architectural materials ex-

A gold-plating copper ox of the Western Xia.

cavated from Western Xia tombs, plus Western Xia ceramics recovered from ancient kiln sites at Lingwu. Articles reflect the history, culture, arts, architecture, and political system of Western Xia.

The Ningxia Hui Minority Peoples' Customs Exhibition

This exhibition displays the customs of the local Hui people. It shows Hui religion, architecture, handicrafts, clothing, eating customs, ceremonies, and wedding and funeral customs.

Exhibition of Stone Rubbings from the Helan Mountains

The Helan Mountains contain a large number of ancient petroglyphs. Rubbings from these, together with color photographs of the designs, show the early presence and activities of northern-steppe nomadic people's customs. These include offerings, hunting, herding, and so on.

The Ningxia Museum currently has around 40,000 items in its collections, which are divided into eight major categories. Notable objects include northern grassland culture animal-style bronze ornaments, Western Han gold, silver and bronze ornaments, Tang-dynasty and Western Xia works of art of various kinds, including the special ceramic technique used during Xi Xia that is known as "raised patterning," done by cutting away extraneous clay from the pattern, and Yuan and Ming-dynasty gilded-bronze Buddhist sculpture.

Yunnan Provincial Museum

Address: Yunnan Province, Kunming City, Wuyi (May 1) Road, #2
Website: www.ynbwg.cn

The Yunnan Provincial Museum is a regional museum, containing around 50,000 objects in its collections. Among these, historical objects account for around 30,000 items of which there are 10,000 bronzes, revolutionary items (7,200), ethnic minorities cultural objects (10,000), handicrafts (4,400). The Museum represents the local nationalities in particular, and features arts from the Nanzhao Dali Kingdom as well as other periods of Yunnan history.

The Yunnan Historical Objects Exhibition has strong regional characteristics, elements that distinguish the local cultures from the Central Plains Han-Chinese culture. Using a diversity of excavated objects, the exhibition displays the face of ancient Yunnan. Many of the objects in this exhibition have important scientific and artistic value, and provide material evidence of mankind's social development.

The exterior of the Yunnan Provincial Museum.

A bronze drum unearthed in Wanjiaba of Chuxiong, Yunnan Province.

Stone Tools

Discoveries from the Yuanmou site in Yunnan are displayed in this exhibition. The fossilized remains of two early hominid teeth, dating from around 1.7 million years ago, were found at the site in 1965. This is the earliest hominid fossil found on the Asian continent to date, and provides extremely important scientific evidence in the research into man's development from primates.

Bronzes

From the Warring States to the Western Han period, the various peoples of Yunnan were creating a distinctive bronze culture. Bronzes excavated at a place called Wanjiapo include the earliest

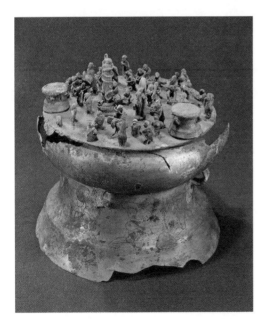

A copper shellfish holding sacrificial utensil of the Western Han dynasty unearthed in Shizhaishan of Jinning, Yunnan Province.

A shellfish holding utensil of Dian nationality with seven oxen and two tigers pattern unearthed in Jinning, Yunnan Province.

The bronze ware exhibition in the Yunnan Provincial Museum.

"Two leopards biting a pig" of the Western Han dynasty unearthed in Shizhaishan of Jinning, Yunnan Province.

A copper peacock.

bronze drums to be excavated in China. Some bronzes from this site have been exhibited in over ten countries around the world, among which are a cow-and-tiger patterned piece that is particularly lively and a cowry-shell container notable for its reflection of slave-society sacrificial practices. Various items reflect the close cultural interaction of Yunnan people with people of the motherland. These include an incense burner that is central-plains in character, a walking lamp, a bronze mirror, a bronze spear, Wuzhu coins, and so on. The seal of the King of the Dian Kingdom in particular testifies to the fact that Yunnan was already an indivisible part of China from some 2,000 years ago.

Yunnan Minority Customs and Ornaments Exhibition

This exhibit displays the dress and ornamentation of some 22 national minorities living in Yunnan, including Dai, Bai, Naxi, Hani, Lahu, Jingpo, Blang, De'ang, Lisu, Pumi, Va, Nu, Drung, Achang, and Jino.

Tracing the Tracks of History

China is an ancient country with an unbroken line of history that extends back some five thousand years. The diverse threads of the historical process have been saved from obscurity by cultural artifacts, by which we can glimpse the accomplishments of our forebears.

National Museum of China

Address: Beijing, Dongcheng District, East Chang'an Street, #16
Web site: www.chnmuseum.cn

The National Museum of China is located on the east side of Tian'anmen Square. It is the largest comprehensive museum in China. The museum's rich collections narrate the history created by the ancestors of the Chinese people over the course of five thousand years.

The National Museum of China was established in 2003 on the twin foundations of the former China History Museum and the former China Revolutionary Museum.

From March of 2007 until June of 2010, the National Museum of China has undertaking renovation and expansion. When finished, the total area of the buildings will be over 192,000 square meters, making this the largest museum in the world. Installation equipment, hardware, and capacities are second to none in the world. The Museum will hold collections totaling over one million objects; there will be over forty exhibition halls. The permanent

The main gate of the National Museum of China.

The design sketch of the new National Museum of China.

exhibitions, titled "Ancient China," and "The Road to Resurgence," will also have more than a dozen special exhibition halls devoted to them as well as international conference facilities.

Once the new National Museum of China is opened to the public, the concept of "museum" and the study of museum sciences will find a whole new expression in China. The level of modernization in the new museum is quite high and expresses the principle that takes "the person as the main focus." Visitors will be able to take what they themselves want to derive from the exhibits, and choose what to view according to their own needs. At the same time, the museum will also provide visitors with various services and places to rest, including a television hall, a study and lecture hall, a theater, a library and materials center, restaurants, programs on transmission of non-physical or non-material culture, and so on.

Ancient China

The earliest items on display here are the teeth of Yuanmou Man from Yunnan Province, dating back some 1.7 million years. The most recent are historical artifacts from the period of the Xinhai Revolution of 1911.

The Early Society Exhibition starts with the Paleolithic period (around 1.7 million years ago to 10,000 years ago), the Early Neolithic period (around 10,000 years ago to 5,000 years ago) and the Late Neolithic period (around 5000 to 4000 years ago). In the Paleolithic section you can see China's earliest "sapiens" called Yuanmou Man, the slightly later Lantian Man, Beijing Man, Jinniushan Man, and also Shandingdong Man. The last had already entered the homo sapiens period. These ancestors wrote the first page in the chapter of China's history. Stone tools that they created, the seeds they collected, bones of the animals that they hunted are all documented in the exhibition cases. The bone-made needle and the teeth and shells that the Shandingdong Man used for jewelry indicate that, by his time, mankind had already begun to sew clothing and have an awareness of aesthetics.

From around 10,000 years ago, mankind began to polish stone tools, make ceramics, weave cloth, and engage in other handicrafts production. The distribution of clans also began to be more widespread. In the exhibit, rice kernels from some 8,000 years ago, bone implements of some 7,000 years ago, and the model of a matriarchal village unearthed in Shaanxi Province from some 6,000 years ago can be seen. From around 5,000 years ago, agricultural techniques were well advanced and besides being able to provide for his own basic needs, man was able to produce a certain surplus. This led to a system of private ownership and the development of classes. At this time, special handicraft industries appeared, also the rudiments of writing, cultural arts and religion. In the exhibits, one can see important ritual implements of the period made from stone and jade.

The slave society was mankind's first class society in history. The exhibition displaying this period is divided into five sections: Xia dynasty, Shang dynasty, Western Zhou, and Spring and Autumn periods, and one that covers all tribes or "nationalities" from Xia to Spring and Autumn.

The Xia (2070–1600 BC) was the first dynasty in Chinese history.

Its center of ruling power was the northern part of what is today Henan and the southern part of Shanxi provinces. The Bronze *jue* and the ceramic cup excavated from Yanshi in Henan indicate that agriculture was a primary economic activity in the Xia period, while the manufacture of bronzes was already quite developed.

The Shang dynasty (1600–1046 BC) was a glorious time of Chinese bronze development. Craftsmen were able to cast very complex shapes and to create highly refined and beautiful inscriptions and ornamentation. The heaviest bronze piece discovered to date is on exhibit here; called the "Simuwu *ding*," which weighs 832.84 kilograms. A four-ram "*zun*" and other representative Shang dynasty bronzes are on display. In addition to bronzes, the manufacture of ceramics, lacquer-making, weaving, jade carving and so on also achieved a certain level of accomplishment. The early-porcelain *zun* excavated at Zhengzhou in Henan is one of the earliest pieces of porcelain found in China to date. Another notable achievement of the Shang dynasty is the ancient script known as *jiaguwen*, or ancient writing on the shoulder-blade bones of oxen and the front plates of tortoises. This writing began the construction of the basic shapes that later developed into "Han" characters.

The Western Zhou (1046–771 BC) was when Chinese bronze-making technology flourished, following the developments of the Shang. In terms of political organization, China adopted a system of division of feudal authority, and a severe system of rites and also punishments was instituted. The ceremonies or rites were used to moderate relations within the ruling class,

A seismograph model.

the system of punishments was used to control and oppress commoners and slaves. Items on display give evidence of these things.

The Spring and Autumn period (770–476 BCE) in China was a period of transition from slave society to feudal society, when the power of the Zhou court greatly declined and some relatively large kingdoms or dukedoms expanded their own influence, initiating a period of intense warfare. The exhibition has representative objects from all the Dukedoms or Kingdoms of the time, and also the world's earliest military tract, excavated in Shandong, called *Sunzi Bingfa*, which is commonly translated into English as "the Art of Warfare."

The final section in this exhibition that reviews early Chinese history shows items from the people on the periphery of the central plains region. These objects have a clearly regional or "outside" quality, and yet they also reflect a relationship between their own locality and the central plains. Representative objects are a dragon-tiger *zun* from Anhui, an elephant *zun* from Hunan, and some ancient Shu bronzes excavated from Guanghan in Sichuan.

The many centuries from the Warring States period (475–221 BC)

A Four-sheep *zun* of the Shang dynasty.

A *ding* with the shape of big broad-mouthed receptacle of the Western Zhou dynasty unearthed in Meixian County, Shaanxi Province.

A 12-character-brick in small seal character of the Qin dynasty that reads "All people are subject to me, every field harvests and everyone can have enough food."

until the Opium War (1840–1842 AD) is regarded as representing a time of feudal society in China. The feudal society exhibit includes seven parts: the Warring States period, Qin, Han, Three Kingdoms-Jin-Northern and Southern Dynasties, Sui, Tang, Five Dynasties, Liao-Song-Western Xia-jin, Yuan, Ming, and Qing. The feudal society exhibit occupies three-fourths of the total China History Exhibit space.

The Warring States period saw unprecedentedly fierce warfare as local states consolidated, and at the same time was a period of rapid economic growth and cultural development. Bronzes of various kinds and coins from many regions are some of the many items on display here.

The Qin period (221–206 BC) reflects the first unified, multi-ethnic, centralized-power feudal period in Chinese history. The period is portrayed by showing some of the Qin soldiers and horses from the famous pit of the First Emperor of Qin, among other items.

To help the visitor understand the power and majesty of the Western Han (206 BC–25 AD) and the expansive power of the Eastern Han (25–220), a number of wall murals, models of sites, and so on are exhibited, together with actual objects from the periods. These show the increasing connections among all continental peoples in the Western Han period.

The Three Kingdoms (220–280), Western and Eastern Jins (265–420), and Northern and Southern Dynasties (420–589) were, in Chinese history, a tumultuous and unsettled time. Yet they were also a period of great advances. The Three Kingdoms, Wei, Shu and Wu, are exhibited in the form of bronzes and ceramics with the ceramics in particular showing a high level of glazing technology in the south.

The Sui (581–618) and Tang (618–907) periods were another time

A Tang-triple-color musical band carrying ceramic camel unearthed in Xiían, Shaanxi Province.

A model of Liao dynasty wood pagoda of Ying County displayed in the National Museum of China.

of great unification in Chinese history. The exhibit reflects the feudal economics of the time, also the increasingly close relations between people of the interior and tribes of the periphery. Exhibited works include items excavated from the grave of Li Jingxun, such Tang *sancai* ceramics as a camel carrying musicians, finely glazed ceramics of *ding-yao*, carved woodblock printed items excavated from Chengdu, and a Guanyin statue of gilded bronze excavated from Zhejiang.

During the Song (960–1279) and Yuan (1206–1368) periods, China's feudal society continued to develop and one clear trait was that the contradictions between Han people and minority

A big copper mirror with double fish pattern of the Jin dynasty unearthed in Acheng, Heilongjiang Province.

A haiyan river zun of the Qing dynasty
(Qianlong Period).

peoples intensified yet economic and cultural relations were strengthened. This can be seen in the various items on display.

The Ming (1368–1644) and Qing (1616–1911) dynasties marked the end of the period of Chinese feudal society. The general trend of this period was general decline and decay in the feudal society, for the 543 years from 1368 with the establishment of the Ming dynasty to Xinhai Revolution of 1911 which overturned the Qing dynasty. The main items in the Ming and Qing part of the exhibition include a Beijing Palace map, porcelains from the Jingdezhen kilns, a Qing-dynasty jade seal, a painting of the Qianlong emperor's southern tour, textile equipment made in England, and the swearing-in document when Sun Yatsen took office as President, the latter being a reproduction.

The Road to Resurgence

This is one of the permanent exhibitions at the National Museum of China. Its grand opening was held on September 25, 2009. More than 1,150 treasures and 980 photographs are displayed in a space of some 2,000 square meters that describe the path the Chinese people have taken in realizing a great resurgence since the Opium War that began in 1840. The exhibition takes a process that occurred over 170 years as its subject.

The historical exhibition on the Revolution of 1911 that overthrew the Qing dynasty.

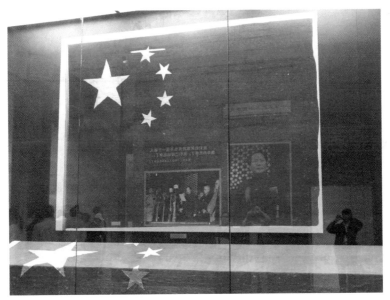

The first national flag of the People's Republic of China flied on Oct. 1, 1949.

Exhibitions include things like the very first flag of New China.

Special Exhibition Halls

The National Museum of China will be opening a number of Special Exhibition Halls that are of the highest standards, including halls for bronzes, ancient ceramics, calligraphy and painting, and ancient Buddhist arts. There will be around a dozen such special exhibition halls.

International Exchanges Halls

After expansion is complete, the National Museum of China will have a number of halls that are devoted to international exchange and understanding. These will include a Hall for Europe, one for Asia, Africa, Latin America and so on. These facilities will use all ways and means to introduce the outstanding civilizations of the world to citizens of China, as well as to display China's longstanding culture to the rest of the world.

Sanxingdui Museum

Address: Sichuan Province, Guanghan City, beside the Yazi River
Website: www.sxd.cn

The Sanxingdui Museum is near an archaeological site that dates to the Neolithic, Shang, and Zhou periods. In 1988, this site was declared a National Key Cultural Relics Protected Unit, due to its size, quantity of material, and the rarity and value of its excavated objects.

The site is north of Nanxing Town of Guanghan City in Sichuan Province. It is mainly located on the higher land between the Yazi River and the Mamu River and it covers 12 square kilometers in total area. The most concentrated parts of the site are at the towns of Sanxing, Rensheng, Zhenwu, and Huilong.

The artifacts from Sanxingdui have had a global impact. In 1986, two large Shang-period sacrificial pits were unearthed with more than one thousand gold, bronze, and jade objects, shocking the entire country and amazing the world. Among other things, the finds proved that Sanxingdui was the capital of the ancient Shu

The external appearance of the Sanxingdui Museum.

Kingdom more than 3,000 years ago. Of all the objects excavated at Sanxingdui, the bronzes are the most fabulous and strange, with their high degree of historical, artistic and scientific value.

Ceramics: Most of the ceramics unearthed at Sanxingdui are made of *"jiashahe"* clay, which has sand in it, and are made on a wheel. They date mainly from four periods. The first dates from some 4,800 to 4,000 years ago, during a representative Neolithic period culture in the Sichuan basin. The second is roughly contemporary with Xia to Shang. The third is contemporary with late Shang, and the fourth with late Shang to early Western Zhou. From the shape, patterning, base, and method of manufacture, the above ceramics represent an unbroken line of development in Shu culture.

Jades: Although not numerous, the techniques for producing these jade objects are fairly advanced and they are well preserved. Among them are ceremonial objects, military objects and tools, with the blades still as sharp as when they were buried. The blades of these objects are so very thin that one can see they were ceremonial in nature and not for actual work or warfare.

Bronze masks.

Gold objects: Not only were the gold objects excavated from Sanxingdui very finely made but they were quite special. They included face masks and various kinds of ceremonial equipment. Among them, a gold staff, with a human head carved on top with fish, birds, and grain is executed in a fine manner with an extremely beautiful pattern.

Bronzes: The Sanxingdui bronzes have been exhibited both inside and outside China and have shaken the field of art history.

A big bronze standing human statue.

The imaginative power of the human statues in particular, their artistic exaggeration, majesty, refinement, and execution make them truly divine works among Shang and Zhou bronzes.

This group of bronzes can be divided roughly into two types. One is ceremonial objects, from whose shapes and artistic styles we can see similarities to surrounding regions. Another type of bronzes is strongly religious in flavor: these constitute religious statues, or idols. Among them is a statue of a standing man who is 2.62 meters high and weighs 180 kilograms. His nose is high and straight, his eyes are large, his forehead is square and he has large ears from which hang pierced earlobes. A long braid hangs down behind his head; he wears a resplendent tall crown on his head, his body is covered with a dragon-and cloud-patterned robe that folds to the left; his left hand is raised, his right arm is folded across his chest, his hands are large, the two feet are bare and he stands on a square pedestal. Among Shang and Zhou bronzes, his shape and manner are absolutely unique.

The superlative excavated bronzes included many bronze heads and face masks. Among these, one mask is 134 centimeters wide and 65 centimeters tall and weighs ten kilograms. If one estimates the full height of a statue with these proportions, it would be an awesome four meters. The mask has large ears and high nose, and exaggerated eyes with protruding pupils.

The grounds and environment of the new museum are exceptionally beautiful. The surrounding space is large and is arranged as in a park, with pools, collections of stones, flowers and trees; the setting also borrows from the natural beauty of the nearby streams.

Jinsha Site Museum

Address: Sichuan Province, Chengdu City, Jinsha Site Road #2
Website: www.jinshasitemuseum.com

The Jinsha Site Museum was built on an archaeological site that was first discovered in early 2001 in an area northwest of Chengdu, Sichuan. It's believed to be the site of the ancient Shu Kingdom's capital after the Sanxingdui culture's disappearance. The entire site covers an area of 30.4 hectares, while total floor space of the museum buildings covers around 38,000 square meters. The museum consists of an Artifacts Hall, Exhibition Hall, Conservation Center, Gardens, and Reception Center.

Construction of the museum started in 2005 and was completed by end-2006. The museum opened to the public on April 16, 2007.

The Artifacts Hall

Located in the eastern part of the museum and on the southern

The Exhibition Hall of the Jinsha Site Museum.

bank of the Modi River, this hall is a steel-frame structure, with a sloping semicircular roof. It rises 19 meters high, spans 63 meters, and has a floor space of 7,588 square meters.

The hall houses the sacrificial zone of the Jinsha Site, which is the most intact of such zones from ancient times found to date in

The sun-and-bird gold foil, which became the logo of China Cultural Heritage on August 16, 2005.

China. Articles recovered from the zone include huge deposits of ivories, numerous items made of gold, bronze, jade and stone, well-preserved "offerings" of the teeth of wild boar and deer antlers, as well as ebony-like wooden blocks. The artifacts are evidence of the rich resources, power, creativity and highly developed handicrafts of the ancient Shu Kingdom. Visitors can sense the grandeur of ritual activities that were held here 3,000 years ago, and can observe how excavations are conducted and how archaeological artifacts are unearthed and conserved.

The Exhibition Hall

The Exhibition Hall on the northern bank of the

The gold face mask.

Modi is a square steel-frame structure, with a sloping roof. It has two stories (three stories in some parts) above ground and one underground, with a total floor space of 16,200 square meters. Visitors follow a declining path in viewing the exhibits, which show the ecological environment, daily life and religious activities of ancient Jinsha, as well as the origin and evolution of ancient Shu civilization.

The four-node jade *cong*.

The bronze statue of a standing man.

Valuable artifacts unearthed at the site are on display. The Hall also has a small high-tech cinema, where visitors can view special films about Jinsha.

Conservation Center

The Conservation Center is located in the northwestern part of the museum, and has a floor space of about 6,800 square meters. It is for the preservation and study of excavated artifacts and for the use of academic exchanges.

The Jinsha Theater near the Conservation Center provides a small venue for artistic performances related to the Jinsha culture.

Zhouyuan Museum

Address: Shaanxi Province, Baoji City, Fufeng County, Famen Town,
　　　　　Shaochen Village

Zhouyuan is an ancient region with more than 3,000 years of history. It is located in the western part of the Guanzhong Plain of Shaanxi Province and includes one of the capitals of the early period of the Zhou Dynasty. In history it is known as "Qi Zhou." The cultural relics both on and below ground are especially rich, and the large quantity of bronzes excavated here are world famous. In 1982, this was declared by the State Council to be a National Key Cultural Relics Protected Unit.

The Zhouyuan Museum was built on the foundation of the excavation of the Zhouyuan site. It was formerly the site of two cultural

The architectural ruins of Zhaochen Palace in Zhouyuan, Shaanxi.

relics Protection and Management Institutes called Zhouyuan Qishan and Fufeng. In 1986 these were combined to become the Zhouyuan Museum which is located in Fugang County, Famen Town, Shaochen Village.

A bronze ware of Zhao King period of the Western Zhou dynasty.

The Zhouyuan Museum's existing exhibitions are divided into indoor and outdoor components. The outside exhibitions are mainly the Village Ancestral Temple and the Shaochen Village Palace, a large-scale architectural grouping. These provide a valuable resource for researching Western Zhou architecture and technology, and the political, economic and cultural systems of the court at that time. These fill what had been a void in ancient Chinese architectural history.

A bronze Shang *you* (wine vessel) of early period of the Western Zhou dynasty.

The indoor exhibitions mainly include the Zhouyuan Excavated Artifacts Exhibit, the Zhouyuan Historical Cultural Relics Exhibit, Western Zhou Calligraphy and Arts Exhibit, Western Zhou Wine-Culture Exhibit, and the special exhibit at Famen Temple which is called the Zhouyuan Precious Cultural Relics Special Exhibit. These exhibits display the some 3,000 items excavated at the Zhouyuan site, including

This *Qiang* plate was a bronze ware made in Gong King period of the Western Zhou dynasty. The bottom of the inside body was engraved with inscriptions of 284 characters.

bronzes, jades, bone, ceramics, tortoise shells and scapula bones used for divination, and so on.

In the exhibition, people can view bronzes from three thousand years ago. One has 284 characters inscribed on the bottom of its interior, relating the history of six previous kings of Western Zhou and the important accomplishments of the seventh king, in power at the time the bronze was made. It also records the family history of the owner of the vessel, providing reliable data for researching Zhou-dynasty history. In the Western Zhou Wine-Culture Exhibition, around one hundred specimens of materials for fermenting alcohol, vessels for fermentation, articles for warming wine, for mixing alcohols and so on are exhibited. China's earliest ceramic-material architectural tiles are also on display, which date to six to seven hundred years earlier than the Qin bricks and Han tiles of Chinese tradition. In the exhibit people can also see valuable Western Zhou *"jiaguwen"* or oracle bone inscriptions, which record the relations between Zhou people and the Shang court as well as other countries. In the calligraphy section, examples of western Zhou calligraphy that have been excavated in recent years are on display.

Mini bone inscriptions of the Western Zhou dynasty unearthed in Zhouyuan, Shaanxi Province.

Suizhou Zenghouyi Tomb Site Exhibition Hall

Address: Hubei Province, Wuhan City, Wuchang District, Donghu Road, #88
Website: www.hubeimuseum.net

The Suizhou Zenghouyi Tomb Site Exhibition Hall is located in the Hubei Provincial Museum. The Hubei Provicial Museum is on the edge of East Lake of Wuchang, which is a very beautiful place and the location of many exhibitions since the opening of the museum. Its collections currently hold some 200,000 objects among which the most astonishing are the objects excavated from the Zenghouyi Tomb.

The Zenghouyi Tomb was built about 2,400 years ago. The rich-

Serial bells or *bianzhong* unearthed in the tomb of Zenghouyi.

A color painted wood carving table screen unearthed in a Chu tomb.

ness of the objects excavated from this tomb and their exquisite beauty have made them world famous. The musical instruments alone have been called an underground musical palace. Among these instruments, the *bianzhong* or bells are most famous. There are 65 bells altogether: 19 *niu* bells, 45 *yong* bells, and 1 *bo* bell. The entire set is capable of performing ancient as well as modern music and Chinese as well as all kinds of foreign music, since their tonal range is broad and the quality of sound is beautiful. The Hubei Provincial Museum made a special exhibition room for this set of *bianzhong*, and at certain times specialists give performances of ancient music for visitors.

Hubei was the center of Chu culture. Inside this Chu tomb were not only Chu items but also rare objects from other countries, such as the kingdom of Yue. A sword belonging to the King of Yue is, for example, one of the renowned treasures found in the Chu tomb.

This bronze *zun* plate unearthed in the tomb of Zenghouyi deserves to be considered a masterpiece of bronze wares of the Warring States period.

Museum of the Terracotta Warriors and Horses of Qin Shi Huang

Address: Shaanxi Province, Xi'an City, Lintong District, Qinling Road
Website: www.bmy.com.cn

A remarkable sight appeared in 1974, near the ancient capital of Xi'an. Some farmers happened to dig up what turned out to be a large-scale pit with terracotta soldiers and horses, belonging to the Emperor Qin Shi Huang, or the Founding Emperor of the Qin. After 2,200 years, the Emperor's tremendous army stood forth as though living again before people's eyes.

The ceramic figures that the farmers found were around the size of real people. The pit was in Shaanxi Province, Lintong County, Jiangzhai Xichang Village. It was around three Chinese *li*, or roughly one mile, from the eastern side of the Emperor Qin Shi Huang's tomb mound. The Chinese Cultural Relics Administrative Department immediately gathered its forces and carried out an investigation. After further excavation they actually found that the area of the discovery was a great deal larger and that inside this

The external appearance of the Museum of the Terracotta Warriors and Horses of Qin Shi Huang.

An archer warrior tomb figure in squatting position.

An armor-wearing warrior tomb figure.

A separate line of foot soldiers in #1 pit.

area were buried some 6,000 terracotta figures of horses and soldiers. After this, archaeologists discovered a second and third pit of horses and soldiers: the first discovery was called #1 pit, nearby in test excavations they discovered pits #2 and #3. Linked together, the three pits covered an area of 20,000 square meters and included around 8,000 figures.

To bury an entire army of individual soldiers under the ground was unheard of. This ancient phenomenon served as evidence of the sophistication and rich cultural heritage of the Chinese people. It is no wonder that the former French Premier expressed amazement when he saw it, "The Qin

The copper horses and horse cart.

terracotta pit is one of the marvels of the world. To go to Egypt and not see the pyramids is not really going to Egypt; to go to China and not see this sight is not really going to China."

In order to better protect this historical treasure house, a building was put over the #1 pit which has a bow-shaped steel framework, to form a vast exhibition hall. The building is 230 meters long, 72 meters wide, and 22 meters high. It can hold two football fields inside. The exhibition halls covering the second and third pits are closed over and of a dome shape, to symbolize the actual form of the tomb of the emperor. The Museum of Terracotta Warriors and Horses of Qin Shi Huang was officially inaugurated and opened to the public in 1979.

Standing inside the hall over #1 pit, people can see over 1,000 of the horses and soldiers that have been excavated and cleaned up;

The battle array in #1 pit.

Terracotta Horses.

the rest of the 5,000 are in the process of being cleaned, one by one. The army is arrayed in a rectangular formation, all facing east. In front are three rows each with 210 warriors making up the front ranks, after them are marching soldiers and horses drawing war chariots, making up the main body of this army. The two sides of the army and the rear each have a line of warriors who face south, north, and west. This was perhaps to maintain flank and rear contingents, to guard against surprise attack.

The terracotta statues, horses and people, are roughly the same size as real horses and people, with proportions that are extremely accurate. This reflects the high level of sculptural arts at the time of the Qin dynasty. From the placement, the hair and clothing styles and weaponry of the statues, one can generally understand their rank and position. Some wear tunics, some carry shields, some have their hair tied in a bun, some wear footwear while others do not, some have armor breastplates, some have fish-scale armor. Soldiers with relatively long beards are placed towards the rear, and one sees at a glance that they are seasoned older generals. In addition to foot soldiers there are also some cavalry members leading horses or driving chariots. Some of the soldiers are kneeling, ready to shoot their arrows: each has a special posture according to his duties.

In terms of finer features, the statues are remarkably lifelike. The head and facial expression of each soldier is different, so that clearly each was the work of a sculptor; they were not produced from a mold. Through fine detail on the eyebrows, face, mouth and nose, the internal character and rich expressions of each soldier are expressed. Some of the statues were clearly northwest minority peoples, which is indicative of the origins of the Qin-dynasty soldiers.

The cavalry and war chariots served an extremely important role in ancient armies. Examples excavated from the pit included steeds that were vigorous and fat. Their ears were erect, their eyes wide and mouths open, they were generally 1.5 meters high, with small-ish heads and relatively short legs. Some people say that these horses seem to resemble the Hequ Horses found in Gansu today, or the Hotan Horses found in Xinjiang, which are known to be excellent racehorses, good at climbing slopes. Clearly, they were also excellent warhorses with great strength.

During the Warring States period, seven powers were at con-tinual war with each other and the competition among their lead-ers led to great advances in weapon design and production. By the time of the establishment of the Qin dynasty, weapons were quite sophisticated. Before this pit was discovered, when only individual examples of Qin weapons were available for research, this was not

Overlooking the Qin Shi Huang Tomb.

More than ten thousand bronze weapons were unearthed from Qin terracotta figure pits and this is a long handle weapon used at that time called "*ji*."

believed to be the case. Once the pit was uncovered and a large number of actual weapons were unearthed, people began to recognize the martial and organizational capabilities of the Qin-dynasty army. Every one of the statues unearthed in the pit had a weapon, and all were actual weapons made of bronze. At the time, the three great kinds of cold weapons (as opposed to what Chinese call hot weapons which came only after the invention of gunpowder) were distant firing weapons, such as bows and arrows, weapons for close-in combat and longer weapons for less close combat. All of these were represented in the pit.

What is most amazing is that these weapons were still shiny and sharp after being excavated. Having been buried over 2,000 years, they had not rusted, except for those that had been crushed and damaged. After rubbing away the mud and dirt, one could imagine that they had just come from a Qin-dynasty craftsman's hands. The production of these weapons was very careful, including cold-casting treatment added to the surface. The weapons were of an alloy made of copper, tin, and lead, but the percentages were different for different categories of weapons and there were micro-quantities of different elements to allow for different hardnesses and elasticity needs. Qin-dynasty craftsmen were in possession of very high metallurgical technology. The blades of the weapons had an oxidized layer and, after scientific evaluation, it was seen that they were put through a salt oxidizing process. This treatment of the surface is a modern technology that was already in use in Chinese weapon production some 2,000 years ago. This thin layer of protection is what kept the weapons from rusting despite being buried for so long.

Changsha Mawangdui Han Tomb Cultural Relics Exhibition Hall

Address: Hunan Province, Changsha City, Dongfeng Road, #50
Website: www.hnmuseum.com

This impressive exhibition hall is located in Hunan Provincial Museum and the tombs and objects that it exhibits date back 2,000 years. Exhibited here are some 3,000 objects from three separate tombs containing the senior Minister of the State of Changsha (Tomb #2), his wife (Tomb #1), and son (Tomb #3). The articles excavated from the tombs have been highly important in researching this very wealthy and sophisticated southern-Chinese culture.

The second room of the hall exhibits lacquer ware, bamboo and wooden objects, agricultural implements, musical instruments,

A piece of "riding clouds embroidery" unearthed from Western Han tombs in Mawangdui, Hunan Province.

Brocade paintings unearthed from #1 tomb in Mawangdui, Changsha.

military implements, wooden figures, silk woven articles and clothes, in addition to three large coffins with their covering paintings, books, and bamboo slips. Among the lacquers excavated from Tomb #3 are cups, saucers, boxes, kettle, tables, screens, and a variety of other objects, totaling some 500 pieces altogether. Among them, most were items of daily use for the lady Xin Zhui while she was alive. These objects had been buried for 2,000 years, and yet are as freshly colored and complete today as when they were new. Tomb #1 produced 48 bamboo cases that held all kinds of agricultural products, fruit, meat, Chinese herbal medicines. Wild game predominated among the varieties of meat. Both Tombs #1 and #3 produced a large quantity of silk fabric. This was analyzed by authorities and included such weave types as *sha, luo, juan, jin,* and *qi,* all of which have great value for the research of ancient Chinese textiles. Ancient Chinese describe silk fabrics as "thin as dragonfly wings, light as fog," and two pieces excavated from Tomb #1, one weighing 48 grams, the other 49 grams, live up to that description.

The family that was entombed in this place was aristocratic. They listened to music in particular, for the musical instruments excavated from the tomb included lutes, bells, flutes, and *se*. The *se* is an ancient Chinese stringed instrument and the one excavated from Tomb #1 had twenty-five strings. The instruments provide important historical material for researching ancient Chinese music.

The occupant of Tomb #3 was a military general. Many weapons were excavated from this tomb but there were also some twenty varieties of books, which incorporate altogether some 100,000 characters. Among the books were volumes one and two of *Lao-zi*, and the *Spring and Autumn Annals*. The earliest volumes of most of these had long since been lost, so the recovery of these early texts has tremendous scholarly value. Among the written materials, a map is a particular treasure as it reflects the quite sophisticated early Chinese understanding of geographic drawing.

The inner coffin of both Xin Zhui's and her son's coffins was covered with a T-shaped piece of painting, which in ancient times was called a *mingjing* and which is similar to what might be called a shroud in the west. Extremely fine paintings were drawn on these pieces of fabric. The conceptual layout of the painting on #1 tomb's fabric was a tri-part division into heaven, the human realm, and

The well preserved corpse of the tomb owner (Xin Zhui) of #1 tomb.

The reconstructed figure of Xin Zhui.

the underground. The colors of the painting are fresh, the strokes are fluid and this is quite rightly considered a masterpiece in ancient art.

Before the Western Han period, China used a burial system of both an inner and outer coffin. Since Xin Zhui was married to very high ranking person, however, she actually used a four-layered coffin. The inner coffins were painted. The second was the most beautiful, employing a black background on which were painted scenes of heaven, including strange spirits and peculiar floating animals.

In the fourth exhibition room one can see the 2,000-year-old female corpse excavated from Tomb #1. A number of preservation measures were adopted during her burial, including burying the coffin very deeply and sealing it tightly so that oxygen, fuel for bacteria, could not enter. Xin Zhui's corpse therefore still had hair, its joints were limber and the soft organs were still soft. At the end of 1972, medical research was carried out on the corpse. The blood-type of the lady was A-type; during her lifetime she suffered from both lung and heart disease.

A visit to this Mawangdui Exhibition Hall will allow the visitor to understand an aristocrat's life at the time of the Western Han dynasty. Not only can one see the actual artifacts, but one can begin to understand the politics, economics, cultural and scientific technologies of the time. The Museum's presentation is a veritable encyclopedia on the Western Han period.

Mancheng Han Tomb Site Exhibition Hall

Address: Hebei Province, Shijiazhuang City, Dongfeng Road #50

Website: www.hebeimuseum.org

The Han-dynasty tomb for which this museum is named was located in a place called Lingshan (Ling mountains), in Mancheng County, Hebei Province. The double tomb held the joint burial of a king of the state of Zhongshan, from the Western Han period, and his wife. The tombs were excavated in 1968. More than ten thousand artifacts were recovered from the two tombs, including gold, silver, copper, iron, jade, stone, ceramics, and lacquer items. The great variety, the extremely fine craftsmanship, and the number of objects were unusual in Han tombs that had been excavated up to

The exhibition in Heibei Museum titled "The homeland of the golden-threaded jade suits: Mancheng Han Tomb."

The golden-threaded jade suit.

that time, making the tomb extremely valuable in terms of its contribution to scholarship.

The Hebei Provincial Museum, located in the city of Shijiazhuang in Hebei Province, organized a special exhibition hall for the Mancheng Han Tomb. In thorough and complete fashion, it has exhibited the various items from the excavation. Over 300 items

The royal lamp of Changxin Palace.

are displayed in an exhibition area of 1,300 square meters. These include utensils of all kinds, for eating, drinking, lighting lamps, lighting the fire, for entertainment, combing the hair, washing, medicine, measuring devices and other tools, weapons, items for chariots, items for setting up tents, painted-pottery ceramics, jades, and stone and glass implements.

This exhibition is considered one of the great treasures of the Hebei Provincial Museum. The golden-threaded jade suit of the occupant of the tomb, Liu Sheng, is rightly world famous. The suit used gold threads to sew together small pieces of jade into a number of separate clothing items, including a face mask, jacket, gloves, pants, and shoes. The gold thread totaled around 1,100 grams, tying together 2,498 pieces of jade. This is the earliest jade suit excavated to date in China, as well as being the most complete. The jade suit of Liu Sheng's wife was similar to that of Liu Sheng. Hers used 700 grams of gold thread and 2,160 pieces of jade.

Inlay-gold bronze Leopard.

A lamp excavated from the tomb is also notable. It was gilded all over and represents a female palace attendant crouching on one knee as she holds the lamp. The space between her right arm and her body is open and is a channel for smoke—the lamp's interior caught the soot from the burning oil, which helped preserve the cleanliness of the room. The gold *"bo-shan-lu,"* or incense burner in the likeness of a mythical mountain, used inset gold to create a cloud-pattern. Its craftsmanship is exquisite. Other items are similarly vibrant and executed with technical skill, giving an idea of the heights of western-Han artistry.

Gilded bronze bottle.

Treasures of China's Stone Grottoes

China's world-famed grottoes can be thought of as an extended art gallery of ancient sculpture, wall paintings, and sutras. Although this gallery is not called a "museum," still it holds some of the rarest and most precious works of art in the world.

Dunhuang Mogao Grottoes

Address: Gansu Province, Dunhuang City, Mingsha Mountain
Website: www.mogaoku.net

The Dunhuang Mogao Grottoes are located some twenty-five kilometers southeast of the city of Dunhuang, Gansu Province. The common name for the grottoes is the Thousand-Buddha caves. These are located on the precipitous face of the east ridge of the Mingsha Mountains. Their construction began in the year 366 AD and, by the time of the Tang-dynasty empress named Wu Zetian, more than one thousand rooms had been carved and painted. Those that have been preserved to this day include rooms from the dynasties of Northern Wei (386–534), Western Wei (535–556), Northern Zhou (557–581), Sui, Tang, Five Dynasties, Song, Western Xia (Xi Xia), and Yuan. In all there are some 492 grottoes, with wall paintings covering 45,000 square meters, and containing 2,415 painted stone carvings. This is considered a priceless artistic trove. It is now protected as a National Key Cultural Relics Protected Unit, and in 1987 it was listed among the ranks of World Cultural Heritage Sites.

There are five levels in all to the Mogao Grottoes, which range from north to south across roughly 1,600 meters. The largest grottoes are 40 meters high and 30 square meters.

The external appearance of the Mogao Grottoes.

The huge mural painting of the Tang dynasty in the #156 grotto: Dunhuang Heroes Zhang Yichao Couple Going on a Journey.

The mural painting Female Performers Playing Music full of flavors of human world in the #122 grotto, and "reverse-playing pipa" is considered the consummate skill among musical dance performances.

The smallest are less than one foot high.

The #16 grotto at Dunhuang is the one that attracted global attention and brought treasure seekers from the West. Two Song-dynasty paintings on its walls show Bodhisattvas on a journey. This is the latest evidence of use of the cave and from this it can be surmised that around the beginning of the eleventh century, when the Xi Xia people invaded this area and conquered Dunhuang, monks at the Mogao Grottoes prepared to flee. They sealed the cave and never returned. For nine hundred years, the room was silently shut off from the world. In the year 1900, when the passageway

A Dunhuang Buddha figure in nirvana.

was being cleaned of debris, this stone archive full of sutras, books, embroideries and sculpture was suddenly discovered. It had some 50,000 items in it and these were later found to include not only a large number of Buddhist sutras, but also Daoist works and works of the Confucian canon. In addition, the cave contained historical records, poetry, literature, information on geography, population, business accounts, calendars and so on. It was discovered to be a full library containing material that documented some ten dynasties, from the Jin in the 4th century to the Song dynasty.

The discovery of the hidden "sutra cave" was a tremendous and startling event for both Chinese and foreign scholars around the

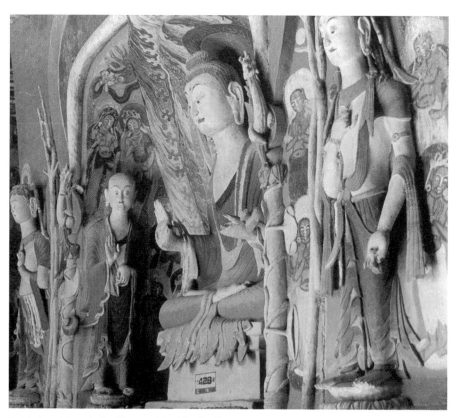

Painted sculptures in the Thousand Buddha Grotto.

A profile of the plank road of the Thousand Buddha Grotto.

The silk painting of the guiding Bodhisattva discovered in the Scripture Hiding Grotto.

world. It attracted extreme attention and as a result was quickly plundered by scholars from England, France, America, Russia, and Japan. In 1943 a Dunhuang Arts Academy was established which began to restore the cave and protect and research its remaining contents.

Dunhuang studies have become an established field of scholarship in many institutions by now, and countless numbers of books and PhD theses have been written about the history and artwork of this extraordinary place. Rather than try to cover the scope of this "museum" here, the reader is encouraged to go and see for himself.

Yungang Grottoes

Address: Shanxi Province, Datong City, Wuzhou Mountain
Website: www.yungang.org

The three main sites in China that are famous for their stone sculpture are Dunhuang, Longmen and Yungang. Among these, the Yungang grottoes are considered first among equals, for their tremendous size, their ancient history, and their relatively complete state of preservation. In 1961, the State Council of China declared the Yungang grotoes a National Key Cultural Relics Protected Unit, and in 2001 the site was listed as a World Cultural Heritage Site.

The grottoes are located 16 kilometers to the west of Datong City in Shanxi Province, on the southern ridge of Wuzhou Mountain. They were carved into the mountain and extend for a kilometer in length. Their carving began in the first year of the Northern Wei

The main gate of the Yungang Grottoes.

A lotus ceiling in the Yungang Grottoes.

dynasty, or 460 AD, and most of the work was finished before the Northern Wei moved its capital to Luoyang in 494 AD although some work continued to the reign of Zhengguang, 520–525 AD. This is the only complete set of Northern Wei stone carving groups in China.

Fifty-three grottoes remain at Yungang today, with some 51,000 statues. The tallest among these is 17 meters high, the smallest is only a few centimeters. Carving techniques have built upon and further developed the traditional arts of the Qin and Han dynasties, but also absorbed the artistic traditions of both India and western regions. The grottoes are divided into three distinct sections, east, central and west, and brief descriptions of those follow.

East Portion of the Grottoes

These are made up of grottoes numbered #1 through #4 ,and are generally called the "tower" caves due to the carved tower or pagoda in the middle of each. All of these were carving during the Northern Wei period, and grottoes #1 and #2 are best preserved. In the center of each is a square tower. Covering the tower as well as all four walls are carved stories of the Buddha and images of the Buddha in various structures. These provide important reference material in researching Northern Wei architecture. The tower in the #3 grotto was not completed before the Northern Wei moved their capital. One Buddha and two Bodhisattva statues were added later and appear to be Tang-dynasty works. The #4 grotto has severely deteriorated but on the southern wall an inscription from the year 520 of Northern Wei has been preserved. This is the last inscription still extant from the Northern Wei period in the Yungang grottoes.

Central Portion of the Grottoes

Numbered #5 to #20, these ar e situated in the central region of the precipice of Wuzhou mountain. They were the earliest part of the grottoes to be carved and they are of the highest value. The five grottoes numbered 16 to 20 were supervised by the high priest under the Northern Wei Emperor Wencheng and are considered to be the most resplendent of all. They are particularly notable for their Buddhist carvings. To the east of these five grottoes are Grottoes #9 to #13, which have come to be known as the "painted" caves since later generations painted the carvings in them. Again, these provide important material for researching the history of architecture, arts, calligraphy and music.

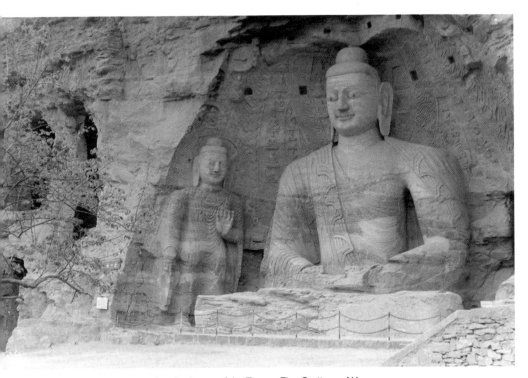

An outdoor sitting Buddha in one of the Tanyao Five Grottoes of Yungang.

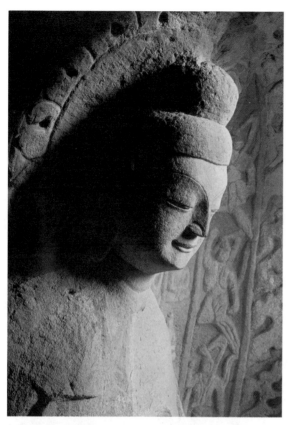

A Bodhisattva figure.

Grottoes #5 and #6 are closely linked and are on a very grand scale: the central seated Buddha in #5 stands seventeen meters high, the tallest of any statue at the Yungang Grottoes. In the #6 grotto stands a 16-meter-high stupa, carved with Buddha statues on all sides. The carving in these two grottoes is very practiced and is considered the pinnacle of the art at Yungang.

West Portion of the Grottoes

To the west of the #20 grotto are relatively small caves, some of which have not yet been given numbers. Right now they number #21 to #53. The dating of these is relatively late, most being works after the 19th year of Emperor Taihe of Northern Wei (495). The carving styles and techniques are more developed than in the eastern and central sections, the Buddha figures are thinner and so on. This is a more Sinified style of Buddhist art, which begins to approach the style of Longmen after the capital of the Northern Wei moved to Luoyang.

The Yungang Grottoes are an open-air museum that attracts the attention of thousands of scholars from around the world every year. The art represented here is of supreme historic and artistic value.

Longmen Grottoes

Address: Henan Province, in the southern outskirts of Luoyang City
Website: www.longmen.com

The Longmen Grottoes are located 12.5 kilometers south of Luoyang in Henan Povince, on both banks of the Yi River. They constitute a world-renowned artistic treasure, now protected as a National Key Cultural Relics Protected Unit and listed as a World Cultural Heritage Site in 2000. The grottoes were begun in the year 494 AD, around the time the Northern Wei Emperor Xiaowen moved the capital to Luoyang. The caves then passed through some 400 years of carving and construction, through the dynasties of East and West Wei, Northern Qi (550–577), Sui, Tang, and Northern Song. The grottoes honeycomb the mountains.

Altogether there are more than 2,345 grottoes at Longmen, with more than 110,000 statues, some 3,600 inscriptions and stelae, and seventy Buddha's stupas. The finest grottoes are the Northern Wei-period Guyang Grotto, the Binyang Grotto, the Lianhua

The well-known "Tablet of Yique Buddhist Shrine" by Chu Suiliang.

Grotto, and the Tang-dynasty Qianxi Temple, among others. Some of the stelaes and inscriptions have become treasures among China's calligraphic arts, including the Tang-dynasty calligraphed work by Chu Suiliang (596–659).

The statues of the Hercules and King of Heaven near the north wall of the Fengxian Temple.

The Binyang Grotto is on the northern part of Longmen Mountain and is composed of three caves. The middle one was begun around 500 AD and was finished in 523, so took twenty-four years to complete. It is recorded that 802,366 craftsmen worked on this grotto. The central Buddha or Sakyamuni and two Bodhisattvas have long, thin faces, and the folds of their clothing is very fine, a characteristic of Northern Wei art. The Lotus-flower or Lianhua Grotto was built in the late Northern Wei period. Its main Sakyamuni is standing and is 5.1 meters tall. The cave is carved with architectural details and floral designs, with scrolling grass patterns, lotus flowers, and so on, all very finely carved. A large lotus flower is carved in high relief on the ceiling.

The Yaofang Grotto, which depicts medicinal cures, is in the northern part of Longmen Mountain. It was begun in the late Northern Wei period and was finished during the Tang-dynasty period of Empress Wu Zetian, so construction lasted around two hundred years. This is the only relatively large cave at Longmen that has

The elaborate works of the Longmen Grottoes.

Northern Qi statues. Some 140 different kinds of medicines and treatments of various illnesses are carved on either side of the cave entryway, which are very important research material for study of China's ancient pharmacopeia.

The Fengxian Temple is at the southern end of Longmen Mountain. It was begun in 672 and completed over the next four years. This contains representative works of Tang-dynasty carving arts. The Vairocana Buddha is huge, and is accompanied by eleven sculptures including disciples, Bodhisattvas, the King of Heaven, Guards and so on. According to the inscription on the sculptures, Wu Zetian helped finance the construction with twenty-thousand *"guan"* of money, and personally participated in leading ministers in the ceremony of "opening the light," i.e. opening the eyes of the Buddha. There is a large stone on the east bank of the Yi River, commonly called the beating-the-drum rock, which is said to be where Wu Zetian played music at the time of the ceremony.

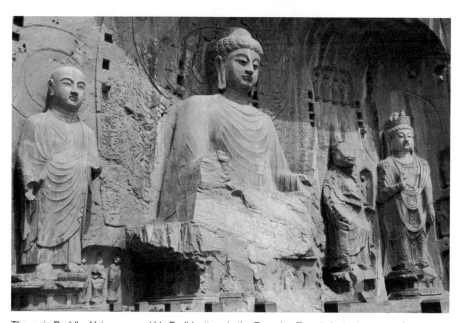

The main Buddha Vairocana and his Bodhisattvas in the Fengxian Temple in the Longmen Grottoes.

Dazu Rock Carvings

Address: Chongqing City, Dazu County, Longgang Town, Beishan Road #7
Website: grotto.cqol.cn

The Dazu rock carvings at Chongqing are one of ancient China's most valuable treasures. They were declared a National Key Cultural Relics Protected Unit in 1961, and in 1999 they were listed as a World Culture Heritage Site.

These carvings are distributed over 41 places in Dazu County, Sichuan. Some 50,000 carvings were begun in 892 AD and carved in the ensuing Five Dynasties and Song, or over a span of some 250 years. In addition to Buddhist and Daoist art, there are also Buddhist, Daoist, and Confucian statues that stand together in one grotto of which the "Mizong" or Tantric (esoteric) Buddhist statues predominate. The largest concentration and largest scale of carvings are at Baoding and

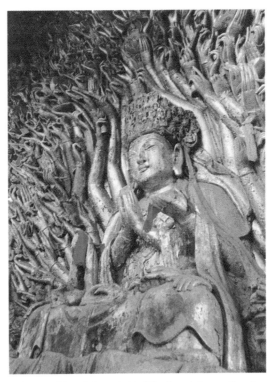

A thousand-hand Guanyin Bodhisattva statue on Baoding Mountain in Dazu.

A Guanxin in charming manner.

Breast-feeding.

A chicken raising lady.

Beishan.

The Baoding carvings are to the northeast of Dazu City, amongst beautiful mountains. Buddhist disciples have traditionally brought incense to the sacred place and there is a saying "look up towards Emei, look down towards Baoding." The Song-dynasty monk Zhao Zhifeng was the instigator of the many Buddhist carvings in this region. Some thirteen places on the mountains hold around ten thousand sculptures that were accomplished over seventy years, from 1179 to 1249. The largest in scale are the Great Buddha Bay and the Small

The sleeping Buddha in the Dazu Rock Carvings Site.

Buddha Bay. In addition to displaying Song-dynasty sculptural art, these are of interest for their narrative appeal: they tell about the birth of Buddha, about the nature of change, about heaven, hell, cause and effect, and especially about people. Normal people, including farmers, are shown working in the carvings, also singing and dancing, drinking wine, pursuing the various tasks of daily life.

Underground Imperial Palaces

The tombs of emperors are a microcosm of the life of the occupant. Objects excavated from them are a kind of living fossil of the history of ancient society. The following section presents only the more famous of the extraordinary number of such microcosms buried in the earth of China.

Tomb of the Yellow Emperor

Address: Shaanxi Province, Yan'an City, Huangling County
Website: www.hdlinfo.com

The Chinese traditional understanding is that the ancestor of the Chinese people is called the Yellow Emperor, and that this Yellow Emperor is buried in the heartland of early China, in what is now the province of Shaanxi. One particular county in Shaanxi lays claim to the burial place of this august being: in 1944, the county changed its name from former Zhongbu County to Huangling (Yellow-tomb) County, in honor of the Emperor.

The Yellow Emperor is believed to have been the leader of the alliance of all tribes in Chinese early society. According to legend, he invented many of China's notable accomplishments such as knowledge of the raising of silkworms, the construction of boats and carts, a system of writing, and the medical arts. For this reason he has long received the love and commemoration of the people.

His tomb is on the northern part of the county seat, on a hill called Qiao Mountain. It is 3.6 meters high, and it has a circumference of around 48 meters. Ancient trees grace the top of the hill and the scenery is lovely. Behind the tomb stands a stele with four large characters that was erected during the Qing dynasty and that commemorates the emperor. To the south of the tomb is a broad terrace, on which to make offerings to the great ancestor.

The tablet of the Yellow Emperor Tomb in Qiaoshan.

Ancient cypresses in the Yellow Emperor Tomb.

At the foot of Qiao Mountain is also a Yellow Emperor Temple, which is also used for offerings and homage. Inside the grounds are ancient bo-trees, some of which may be upwards of one thousand years old. Among them is one tree that stands 19 meters high and whose branches are some ten meters long. Legends say that it was planted by the hand of the Emperor himself. Before the great hall of the Temple are around 70 stelae recording the offerings made by dynasty after dynasty of emperors and kings who came to make offerings. In the center of the Great Hall entryway hangs a plaque extolling the Yellow Emperor as the creator of writing, and therefore the earliest ancestor to lead Chinese into a civilized age.

People who come to pay respects at this temple can perhaps begin to understand the significance of this ancient person to the Chinese. He brought blessings upon the land through his outstanding achievements.

The Xuanyuan Temple commemorating Yellow Emperor.

Maoling Museum

Address: Shaanxi Province, Xingping City
Website: www.maoling.com

Maoling is located in Xingping City of Shaanxi Province, and is the tomb of the Han Emperor Wudi (also known as Liu Che). Construction of the tomb was begun in 139 BC, and the tomb has been declared a National Key Cultural Relics Protected Unit. The Maoling Museum includes the tomb and exhibition halls of relevant cultural artifacts and architecture. It covers some 120,000 square meters with a building area of 16,000 square meters. The style of the building copies that of contemporary Han-dynasty houses.

The Maoling Museum currently has two exhibition halls. The eastern exhibits rare objects recovered from the Yangxin Tomb; the western has a permanent exhibit showing the historical artifacts of Western Han. The Western Han artifacts in both halls total 320 pieces, all of them excavated from within the precinct of the protected area around the

A gold-plating copper horse of the Western Han dynasty displayed in the Maoling Museum.

The stone carving "Horse trampling the Xiongnu" in front of the Huo Qubing's Tomb.

Maoling Tomb. Very rare objects constitute around one third of the total.

The carved stelae and sculptures of General Huo Qubing's tomb are one of the museum's main attractions. These were done at the time and accompanied the burial of the emperor. Their artistry rivals such other well known Western-Han pieces as the "Horse Trampling the Xiongnu" sculpture: they occupy a significant place in the art history of world sculpture.

At present there are 4,100 objects in the collections of the museum. Most of these date from the early period of Western Han. Part of their value lies in their diversity and quantity, the fact that they were "*ming-qi*" or used to accompany the tomb occupant, and the fact that they include a substantial number of items of daily life so that they help reveal the life and customs of the region at that time. The Maoling objects were executed with a high degree of craftsmanship and have the special Western-Han quality of being vital and confident.

Qianling Museum

Address: Shaanxi Province, Xianyang City, Qianxian County
Website: www.sn.xinhuanet.com/200706mon/ql.htm

The Qianling Tomb was built for the third Tang-dynasty emperor and his empress, who were buried together. The third emperor was Li Zhi and his empress was Empress Wu Zetian. This is the most representative among the eighteen Tang-dynasty tombs and is the best preserved. It is located on top of Liang Mountain, six kilometers north of Qianxian County in Shaanxi Province, around eighty kilometers from Xi'an. The scale of the tomb is very large with the precincts of the tomb and gardens totaling an area of 2.4 million square meters.

What one mainly sees today on the grounds of the Qianling Tomb are extremely beautiful stone carvings that stand on top of the hill. They are arrayed in a line leading from the "crimson sparrow gate" to the north and mark the "way of horses and grooms," the double line of statues leading up to the tombs.

The first pair of stone carvings is symbolic and indicates that

Stone human statues outside the Qianling Tomb.

The stone carving "Winged horse" standing in front of the Qianling Tomb.

this is a tomb; then come a pair of war steeds and crimson swallows. The steeds have cloud-pattern curling on their haunches, as though they were flying amidst the clouds. The crimson sparrow is depicted using high relief, with strong, beautiful carving. According to legends at the time, this mythical bird was sent as a funeral gift from the king of what is now Afghanistan. It carried the symbolic meanings of both homage and protection, and so was carved into the stone before the tomb.

Next come five pairs of stone horses, on which are carved saddles, stirrups and other equine accouterments. Originally each pair had stone grooms leading them but now only three remain. Behind the horses are ten pairs of retainers waiting on the emperor. They wear tall crowns and have broad-sleeved long robes that are belted at the waist. Their hands hold daggers and they look forbidding as they guard the tomb.

Two rows of stone stelae come next, with one on the right that is blank: it holds no characters or writing. This was put up on the orders of Empress Wu Zetian just before she died. She noted that her merit surpassed what later people could judge, and so they were not to write anything at all. The stele stands 6.3 meters high, and 2.1 meters

The tablet of "No words" for Empress Wu Zetian.

A mural painting in the tomb of Princess Yongtai in the Qianling Tomb.

wide, 1.49 meters in depth. Another stele, in contrast, holds some 8,000 characters, all of which were inlaid in gold after being carved so that their message could shine out over the empire. The text extols the civilized rule and military power of Emperor Gaozong.

Behind the stone tablets on the right side of the horses and grooms way is a row of sixty-one stone statues of men. Almost all of their heads have long since been destroyed, but two remain to show us what they once looked like: these men had high noses, deep-set eyes, and were clearly people of Central Asia.

Two stone lions standing before the crimson swallow gate represent the finest works of sculpture at the Qianling Tomb. These are very large and ferocious: with curling fur, protruding eyes, open mouth and sharp teeth, they bristle with all the authority and power of the Tang dynasty.

According to historical documents, a number of accompanying tombs surrounded the Qianling imperial-tomb precinct. These were mostly robbed in antiquity but certain superlative works of art remain that can be seen at this museum. It is well worth a visit.

Dingling Museum

Address: Beijing, Changping District, Special Area of the 13 Ming Tombs
Website: www.mingtombs.com/jqyl/dl

The Dingling Museum is located in Changping County at the foot of the Yanshan Mountains, outside Beijing. This is the site of the world-famous Ming-dynasty "Thirteen Tombs" and the "Dingling" counts as the tenth among those thirteen. The thirteenth emperor of the Ming dynasty is buried here, together with his two empresses. Zhu Yijun was the Shenzong Emperor, with the reign name of Wanli. He ascended the throne at the age of ten, in 1572, and was on the throne for 48 years. His was the longest reign of any Ming-dynasty emperor.

Overlooking the Dingling Tomb.

The portrait of the Ming Emperor Shenzong, Zhu Yijun, who was buried in the Dingling Tomb.

A dragon robe unearthed from the Dingling Tomb.

Construction of the Dingling tomb was begun in 1584 and was finished in 1590. The cost was said to be eight million *liang* (tael) of silver; the tomb stands on 18 hectares of land. The main buildings are built along an axis that includes a stone bridge, stelae tower, gates, halls, tower, surrounding wall and the underground palace hall. The surface buildings were destroyed several times by fire, so except for the *minglou, baoding*, wall, and underground palace which have been relatively well preserved, only traces of the other buildings remain.

In May of 1956, archaeologists found the entryway to the underground palace at a depth of 27 meters. Blocking the way stood the "vajra wall" gate, which stands 8.8 meters high. In the gate was a doorway shaped like the Chinese character for "man." This entryway was tightly sealed with twenty-three layers of large bricks. Tearing down this human-shaped entryway in the gold steel wall, archaeologists followed along the corridor inside and encountered two large carved-jade doors. These were three meters high, and each of the two swinging doors in the frame was 1.8 meters wide and weighed around four tons. Nine rows of symbolic knobs were carved on each. A bronze beam of around ten tons in weight was set across the top part of the door: the axles of the doors were set in

An emperor's gold crown unearthed in the Dingling Tomb.

An empress's phoenix crown unearthed in the Dingling Tomb.

this so that they could swing open. Beyond the doors was an underground palace hall containing a suite of connected rooms, including front, middle, rear, left and right chambers. All were spacious and separated by seven stone gates. The front and middle halls used "gold bricks" as a floor covering, the others were of stone construction.

The rear chamber was the main part of the palace. Three coffins lay here, with Zhu Yijun in the middle and his two empresses on either side. Twenty-six red-lacquered cases were set around the coffin, holding some 3,000 items made of gold, silver, gems, ceramics, jades, and fabric, all to accompany the burial.

All of the Dingling Museum's collections come from articles unearthed from this underground palace. They are not only beautiful, they represent a valuable resource for studying Ming court life and Ming craftsmanship.

Among items excavated from Dingling are the emperor's crown and a phoenix crown that are particularly notable. The golden crown is woven of very thin threads of gold and two golden dragons are crouched and coiled on top. The crown is 24 centimeters high with a diameter of 20.5 centimeters and a weight of 826 grams. The phoenix crown was used by the empress when she received visitors at court. It uses lacquered bamboo and silk as a base and on top are silk gold dragons and a jadeite phoenix, as well as flowers that are created out of gems. The crown is encrusted with 150 precious gems and more than 5,000 pearls.

Qing Dongling and Qing Xiling Tombs

Address: Qing Dongling—Hebei Province, Zunhua City, Malan Yu Qing
        Qing Xiling—Hebei Province, Yixian County, below Yongning
        Mountain
Website: www.qingdongling.com
        www.qingxiling.com

The Eastern Tombs, or Dongling, of the Qing dynasty are located
in Zunhua City in Hebei Province. They rest in the Malan Valley of
the Changrui Mountains, some 125 kilometers from Beijing. The
fifteen tombs located here include those of certain Qing emperors
who reigned from 1644 onwards, including the tomb of the great
Kangxi emperor. The tomb of the famous Cixi Dowager Empress
is also located here. The fifteen tomb-mounds represent the largest
and most complete grouping of imperial tombs that still exist in
China today. They are arrayed east and west along the southern-
facing slope of the southern ridge of the Changrui Mountains. The
central axis of each tomb faces northward, towards a backdrop of
mountains. The site is extremely beautiful, with ancient pines and
long spirit ways gracing the approach to the royal resting places.

The heart of the Eastern Tombs is the tomb of Emperor Shunzhi,
a tomb that is called Xiaoling. A total of five emperors, fifteen
empresses, and 136 concubines are buried at the Eastern Tombs
and all of these, with one exception, are arrayed to the east and
west of this centrally located Xiaoling. The tomb of Kangxi is situated to the east and slightly south of Xiaoling. It was begun in the
20th year of Kangxi's long sixty-year reign, and its size and scope
are second only to Xiaoling. The tomb of Qianlong is set to the
west of Xiaoling in the Shengshui Valley. It is a joint burial of the
emperor, his two empresses, and three concubines. It too is a very
special underground palace, with three rooms and four entryway

The Qing Eastern Tombs in Malan Valley in Zunhua City, Hebei Province.

gates; it reaches a depth of 54 meters and occupies 327 square meters of space. One notable aspect of this tomb is that all of its walls and ceilings are completely covered with stone carvings relating to Buddhism. Several tens of thousands of characters of Buddhist scriptures also adorn the tomb, written in the clear and fluid lines of Sanskrit and Tibetan scripts.

The tomb of Empress Dowager Cixi contains the most accomplished above-ground artistry of all the Qing-dynasty tombs. It includes refined and exquisite stone carving that depicts phoenixes and dragons cavorting amongst clouds. The splendor of the architecture is unique, with gold foil fixed to the ceiling, superb painting, and fine carpentry of the actual structures. The tomb-chamber of Cixi has already been "opened" and is the only tomb of an express's underground palace that has been excavated to date.

Four of the Qing-dynasty imperial tombs are located some 120 kilometers to the west of Beijing, in Hebei Province. These are known as Xiling or Western Tombs. This is where Emperor Yongzheng selected a site and began to erect his resting place. Eventually the location came to include the burials of three empresses, four emperors, and a number of princes, altogether 76 people in fourteen tomb groupings. Above-ground extant buildings occupy 50,000 square meters.

The organization of Xiling or Western Tombs is similar to the

The Qing Western Tombs in Yixian County, Hebei Province.

Eastern. Yongzheng's tomb, called Tailing, sits in the middle. The others are arrayed to his east and west. The spirit way leading up to Tailing is five *li* in length, or nearly two miles, and sculptures on either side are impressive. In the neighboring area twenty-one of Yongzheng's concubines are buried, also his empress, the blood mother of Qianlong.

To the west of the Tailing tomb of Yongzheng are two imperial groupings, one of which belongs to Emperor Daoguang. This includes buildings that are unique for not being painted but rather carved in dragon designs from *nanmu* wood. The dragons cover every inch of space on the ceiling, and the pillars and beams are alive with swimming dragons, coiled dragons, vigorous dragons.

To the east of Tailing is the most recent tomb among the western-tomb groupings, which was built for Guangxu and his empress. It is called Chongling. Groundbreaking began in the first year of Xuantong (1909) and the work was completed in the fourth year of Minguo (1915). This was the last imperial tomb among all of China's imperial tombs and it holds Guangxu and his empress. This was robbed in early years, but when restoration and research of the site began in 1980 some jades and pieces of silk were found. Near the Chongling tomb are the tombs of various concubines.

All of these tombs have been declared National Key Cultural Relics Protected Units, and are listed also as World Cultural Heritage.

Hua-xia Civilization

It goes without saying that China is a large country, with an ancient and well-developed civilization. Cultural aspects of "*hua-xia*," such as silk, tea, ceramics, and Chinese medicine, have all made great contributions to mankind. Note that the term "*hua-xia*" is broader in meaning than "China." It indicates more of a cultural space than a geographic designation, and also implies a historical lineage. "*Xia*" is the name of the first-known dynasty of what later came to be "China," dating to some three millennia ago. The term "*hua*" includes both overseas Chinese as well as non-ethnic Chinese under the overarching umbrella of what today is known as China.

China National Silk Museum

Address: Zhejiang Province, Hangzhou City, Yuhuang Shan Road #73-1
Website: www.chinasilkmuseum.com

The China National Silk Museum is in Hangzhou, on a hill called Jade-Emperor Mountain that lies at the southern end of the lake. Including the grounds, the Museum covers an area of 73 *mu* (a Chinese unit of area that equals 0.1647 acres,) and the building space covers 8,000 square meters. The complex of buildings is somewhat fan-shaped, or curved like a bow. A statue of the legendary goddess of silkworms, Lei Zu, stands in front. The building holds 3,000 square meters of exhibition space. In 2003, a thorough renovation of the exhibitions resulted in a new way of presenting the material. The main hall narrates the story of silk in China. This includes the early sources and development of silk production, the main kinds of silk fabric, a bit about the Silk Road, and the role that

The external appearance of the China National Silk Museum.

An ancient jacquard silk weaving machine.

silk played in ancient life and society. The "dyeing hall" and the "contemporary accomplishments hall" display the development of the loom in China as well as the silk industry after New China was founded, and accomplishments as a result of research and development and foreign trade.

The first thing that greets the visitor in the entry hall to the museum is a large model of a Song-dynasty loom. Around its base is reproduced a Song-dynasty painting (done for the emperor Song Gaozong) that depicts mulberry raising and silk weaving. The original of this painting is more than five meters long and was done by a court artist for the emperor. Through linked-painting technique, it systematically portrays the entire process of making silk, from planting mulberries and raising silkworms to unraveling the silk from cocoons and weaving cloth.

The Silk Fabrics Hall exhibits a large number of ancient silk artifacts, as well as models and photographs. Articles from the Neolithic period include certain items from more than 4,700 years ago, and even a dyed piece of silk woven fabric from more than 5,600 years ago. Woven silk pieces excavated from the Jiangling Mashan Chu Tomb in Hubei Province show the high level of weaving technology during the Warring States period.

By the Han period, the development of Chinese silk weaving had reached its first peak. The fabric excavated from the #1 Tomb at Mawangdui that is exhibited here is extraordinary. It lay underground for more than 2,000 years and yet is still as lustrous and beautiful as when it was buried.

During the Tang dynasty, silk weaving entered a period of innovation due to extensive east-west cultural exchange. The pieces excavated from a group of tombs at Astana in Turpan, Xinjiang, exhibit the artistic style of those times. Printing-on-silk technology was highly developed during the Tang period. All of the printing technology methods that we have today were already in existence at the time, and some of these are exhibited here.

A pair of silk skirt-style trousers of the Song dynasty.

Woven silk fabrics in the Song and Yuan dynasties include numerous weaving techniques that are both complex and very beautiful. Weaving with gold came to be one of the more refined techniques and some pieces are displayed that were excavated from a site in Inner Mongolia. Silk brocades were used in the Song and Yuan periods but were most vibrant in the Ming and Qing dynasties. Exhibited here are a number of brocade items that were worn by emperors, empresses, and senior officials.

The Silkworms and Mulberry Hall exhibits the entire process of cultivating silkworms. On display are materials about some live mulberry trees in China that are over one thousand years old. The life cycle of a silkworm is shown, and specimens from around the country are on display. One can watch the birth and growth of the little worm, the way it spits out the silk and creates its own cocoon and the way that cocoon is then unwound to create silk threads. The Silk Production Hall gives the history of the tools of the trade. The Weaving Hall displays all kinds of traditional looms and allows visitors to actually sit at a loom and try for themselves. The Dying Hall has specimens of many kinds of plants and minerals that were used in traditional dyes. Nearby is also a small botanical garden that raises some of the plants used for these dyes. In addition to displaying the processes of dying, printing and embroidery, demonstrations are given by masters on the spot of the various techniques.

China National Tea Museum

Address: Zhejiang Province, Hangzhou City, Longjing Road, Shuangfeng
          Village
Website: www.teamuseum.cn

The China National Tea Museum is at West Lake in Hangzhou. It is composed of four separate buildings, each with a separate form and function. The first, a two-story building, contains exhibition halls.

This building displays the history of tea, and includes six sections on tea implements and tea customs. The Tea History Hall begins with a section on Lu Yu (733–804), a Tang-dynasty figure who is revered as a tea saint and who excelled in the Way of Tea. A chronology of tea then systematically gives the development of tea in China, from Yunnan trees, to seeds, to growth of the industry. A

The exterior of China National Tea Museum's Exhibition Hall.

following hall displays all kinds of tea-processing methods that result in green tea, black tea, white tea, flower tea, pressed tea, Oolong tea and so on. These are accompanied by photographs from tea-growing regions of China.

A wood carving statue of the ancient tea sage—Lu Yu—displayed in the China National Tea Museum.

The Tea Affairs Hall introduces the planting, plucking, processing, preserving, and steeping of tea, all the various technologies that have to do with tea. The exhibition shows historic processing as done in the Tang and Song dynasties, but also has photographs of modern tea factories and models of modern tea-processing factories. In this hall are also modern methods of testing, connoisseurship about tea waters, and so on. The concluding portion of this hall displays photographs and information that describes the beneficial health effects of tea.

On the second floor are the Tea Implements Hall and the Tea Customs Hall. The treasures of the museum are located here. Some two hundred exquisite objects are displayed that were used as tea implements from early times to now. They include bowls, trays, bottles, kettles, cups, and so on. Song-dynasty ceramics include various famous glazes of the period, Ming-dynasty and Qing-dynasty pieces include imperial examples from the Palace Museum. Some items on display are from Japan, and there are a number of tea objects from Korea. One particularly noteworthy object is a large tea kettle used during the Minguo period (1912–1949). It stands some seventy centimeters high and has a diameter of around fifty centimeters and is an example of kettles that were in common use in Minguo tea houses.

The Tea Customs Hall shows scenes from five main tea-drinking regions of China. It reveals the variety of customs that have grown up around the culture of tea. Tibetan tea-drinking is shown here, for example, with a full set of implements and tea-related objects. A traditional scholar's tea-making arrangements are displayed. From Jiangnan or south of the Yangtze, the Han people's tea-drinking customs are shown. From Yunnan, a bamboo pavilion is recreated that shows bamboo-segment tea containers and other tea-drinking customs of people in Xishuangbanna. There are also examples of gong-fu tea from Chaozhou, Guangdong, covered-bowl tea from Sichuan and so on.

The third building in the Tea Museum, which is set off by itself, contains five rooms with different and appropriate décor for serving different kinds of tea. The visitor can enjoy Japanese tea in a Japanese tearoom, Yunnan tea in a bamboo pavilion, Ming-dynasty tea in a Ming-dynasty teahouse. Guests are welcome to enjoy the variety and pleasures of tea.

Jingdezhen Ceramics Museum

Address: Jiangxi Province, Jingdezhen City, Xishi District, Fengshu Shan, Panlong Gang
Website: www.jxmuseum.cn/jxww/dsbwg/jdztc.htm

This museum is located in the Panlong Mountains, outside the city of Jingdezhen in Jiangxi Province. Panlong means "curling dragons," and the location of the museum is an ancient site for ceramic production in China that used the mountainsides for what are known as dragon kilns. The museum was built in 1980.

The earliest ceramics at Jingdezhen trace their history back more than 1,700 years, but the height of the fame and technology of

Jingdezhen kilns came during the reigns of Kangxi, Yongzheng, and Qianlong in the Qing dynasty.

In addition to continuing the traditions of earlier successful glazes and techniques, many new forms of ceramic technology were invented here. Some are celebrated overseas, although few foreigners know their source. All of these are on display at the museum. The architecture of the Museum (the name of which has changed from the former Jingdezhen Ceramics History Museum) is in Ming and Qing style: buildings include display halls, workshops, glazing areas, stores, residences, a library, administrative areas, and other structures.

The "Qing garden" includes one group of buildings within the museum area that lie in a secluded and quiet forested valley. It copies a famous Qing-dynasty structure called the Yuhua Tang, with traditional construction and carving. The décor is simple and elegant, and the building contains some ancient stone horses as well as some of the ceramics described below. Visitors to the Jingdezhen Ceramics Museum are attracted most to exhibits of valuable ancient ceramics but also to the demonstrations of techniques by which these ceramics were originally made.

In the great hall of the Yuhua Tang some of these valuable ceramics are on display. They include recently excavated ex-

Egg-shell china.

An ancient porcelain kiln.

The blue-and-white porcelain.

A porcelain statue.

amples of Ming-dynasty pieces from the reigns of Yongle and Xuande. The glazes are lustrous and soft, the pieces are dated with reign marks and are masterpieces of the art at the time, with tremendous artistic as well as scientific research value.

In neighboring simple and unadorned handicrafts workshops, craftsmen use ancient implements to demonstrate traditional arts. Focusing single mindedly on making beautiful replicas, they demonstrate the entire process of creating ceramics. More than 150 older artisans, together with a younger generation that is carrying on the tradition, can be seen kneading clay, fashioning vessels, applying underglazes. The production process is basically the same as was recorded in Ming and Qing period histories. The workshops are themselves works of art, for they are replicas of the ancient ceramics craftsmen's actual architecture. The entire presentation represents the most complete set of handicrafts systems that has been come down to us from the Qing dynasty.

Huqingyutang Museum of Traditional Chinese Medicine

Address: Zhejiang Province, Hangzhou City, Dajing Xiang, #95
Website: www.hqyt.com

At #95 Dajing Xiang in Hangzhou is one of the rare remaining commercial establishments from the late Qing period that is in its original condition. This is the famous southern-Chinese medicine house of Hu Qing Yu. Today, this house has been restored and made into China's first Chinese pharmacopoeia museum.

It is said that the predecessor to Hu Qing Yu was a medicaments maker in the southern Song dynasty. By the time of the Tongzhi 13th year of the Qing dynasty (1874), an Anhui businessman named Hu Xueyan (1823–1885) built the national brandname of Hu Qing Yu on this foundation, and in the process started China's most famous pharmacy.

Stepping over the simple doorjamb and through an austere door, one passes through a corridor on which hang many illustrations of fables and tales that relate to the medicaments of the house. On the opposite wall are hung more than thirty brand names of famous medicines. Once one reaches the great hall of the actual enterprise, a gold-lacquered wooden high

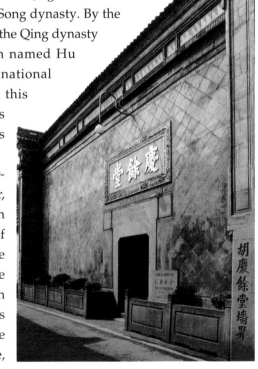

The medicine house of Hu Qing Yu.

A long corridor full of boards that introduce all kinds of medicine.

counter is always one's first impression. Behind it is a cabinet "of a hundred eyes," holding many small drawers which hold as many potent remedies.

The rear room of the enterprise was used by what were called counter-watchers, the accountants who tallied up the actual transactions. This was the main place for selling the goods. Today it has become the Traditional Chinese Medicine Museum exhibition hall. All kinds of ancient implements and artifacts used in the conduct of the herbal medicine business are on display here. Further back in the building is where the medicine was made. Herds of deer were once kept behind the house, that were used in the making of the medicine known as Meihua Lu. Before a deer was killed, a sign would be hung out to advertise this fact and to attract people to come watch, in order to prove that Hu Qing Yu used only authentic materials in its "Deer Pills."

Hu Qing Yu's ancient architecture not only has historical

Traditional pharmaceutical tools collected by the medicine house of Hu Qing Yu—a gold shovel and a silver pan.

The inscribed board that reads ìNo cheatingî inscribed by the shop owner hung in the shop.

The interior gate of the business hall of the medicine house of Hu Qing Yu.

and artistic value, but it is also interesting in terms of the history of the business. It is said that Hu Xueyan did some calculations and figured out that building this establishment would cost him 200,000 taels of silver. He reckoned that each year he would expend 2,000 taels, but still the income brought in by just having this building would far outweigh the cost of any other method of advertising. This was Hu Xueyan's rationale for building a quite expensive and handsome building. Anyone who came to his store would become a mouthpiece to advertise his wares: they would all take on the duty of promoting Hu Qing Yu. The logic seems to have worked.

Quanzhou Maritime Museum

Address: Fujian Province, Quanzhou City, Donghu Street, #425

Website: www.qzhjg.com

The new Quanzhou Maritime Museum was built in 1990 on Donghu Street. It has four exhibition halls: "Quanzhou's maritime relations in ancient times," "Quanzhou religious stone sculpture," "Quanzhou oceangoing vessels," and "Quanzhou maritime people's cultures." In 2003, an exhibition hall was built to the east of the main hall, which is called the "Quanzhou Islamic Culture Exhibition Hall." There is also a "Quanzhou Ancient Ships Exhibit" located in the old Kaiyuan temple. Together, the two locations of the museum cover 35,000 square meters, and the exhibition space approaches 9,000 square meters.

The Quanzhou Ancient Ships Exhibit is located on the east side

The exterior of the Quanzhou Maritime Museum.

The model of a restored sea boat of the Song dynasty unearthed in Quanzhou.

A sea boat of the Song dynasty unearthed in Houzhu Port in Citong, Fujian.

of the Kaiyuan Temple. A total space of 1,307 square meters is divided into the reception hall, the ships hall, and a hall for artifacts that have been excavated from ocean-going vessels. The reception room has the aspect of a harbor. The ancient remains of a ship that is 24.2 meters long and 9.15 meters wide are exhibited here and constitute one of the most important of the exhibits.

A tablet display of Arabic denizens who lived in Quanzhou in the Song and Yuan dynasties.

Items excavated from oceangoing vessels are displayed on the second floor. Exhibited are things from shipwrecked ocean vessels that have been recovered, including a Song dynasty ship that was excavated in 1982—the objects that accompanied that Fashi ship are displayed here as well as a 1 to 10 model of the ship itself.

The "Quanzhou's maritime relations in ancient times" exhibition hall is divided into chronological sections by dynasty. These display the circumstances surrounding Quanzhou's ancient commerce. The Quanzhou religious sculptures are located

Quanzhou Chinawares sold for abroad of the Song and Yuan dynasties—"junchi."

in the east exhibition hall. Around 300 sculptures are on display that were left in Quanzhou and passed on to later generations by religious representatives of the Song and Yuan periods. Religions represented include, most importantly, Islam, also Nestorian Christian, and various religions from India.

More than 140 ship models are exhibited in the China World Ship Exhibition Hall. Included are all kinds of ships that navigated the Changjiang (Yangtze River), the Yellow River, all kinds of warships, ancient emissary's ships, as well as lavish cruise ships. The ships used by the famous Zheng He are displayed here, as well as Zheng Chenggong and the ships used by colonialists in their naval battles. In addition, ships have been assembled here from all kinds sources, such as the Taiwan Ya-mei ship, cow-hide ships from Tibet, Sheepskin boats from the Yellow River, single-log ships, and so on.

The Quanzhou Maritime Museum currently has a total of 10,000 objects in its collections. Among these, 102 objects are first-grade cultural relics. Of these, the ancient articles excavated from ancient ships and the religious sculptures are considered most valuable. Among the collections of this museum are also some that relate to the history of overseas Chinese, and there are also Spanish silver coins and such foreign articles from the time when Quanzhou's overseas-relations were at their height.

Assembly of Talents: Arts and Literature

China has made outstanding contributions to the world in more than just the material realm. It has also made contributions in the area of spiritual [or "mental"] civilization: it is an ancient Eastern country with a highly refined human culture. The following institutions highlight different aspects of this culture.

National Art Museum of China

Address: Beijing City, Dongcheng District, Wusi (May 4) Street, #1
Website: www.namoc.org

The National Art Museum of China is located on May-Fourth Street in Beijing (Wusi Dajie). It is a national-level art museum that concentrates on works by China's modern painters. The Museum covers a total area of 30,000 square meters, with a building area covering 18,000 square meters. The five floors of the Museum have a total of 17 exhibition rooms, with an exhibition area of 8,300 square meters. The "exhibition line" is 2,110 meters long. After renovation and expansion, the new museum is quite handsome.

The corridor and courtyard of the National Art Museum of China.

The National Art Museum of China collects, conserves, displays, and researches superlative artworks of modern Chinese artists and also folk art. It organizes a variety of Sino-foreign exhibitions, sup-

The exhibition hall of the National Art Museum of China.

The facade of the National Art Museum of China.

ports academic exchange and research, and publishes collected works as well as essays on art theory. It has more than 100,000 objects in its collections that encompass modern and contemporary art and people's folk art. Some ancient paintings are also held in the collection, as well as some works of art from other countries.

As a cultural focal point for both Chinese and foreigners, the Museum puts on many types of exhibitions. Other than the permanent exhibitions organized by the museum itself and jointly sponsored exhibits from other museums, it also holds short-term exhibits that explore "brave new initiatives" and give exposure to different Chinese regions. In order to heighten international communication in the arts arena, the Museum often holds exhibitions brought in from other countries. The collections of the Museum have also been abroad on exhibition many times. Every year, the Museum holds more than 100 exhibitions in Beijing, and every year it receives several million visitors. The exhibition on Dunhuang arts, which was held in 2008, broke three records for daily attendance, monthly attendance, and single-exhibit attendance. In the space of two months, 660,000 visitors saw the show.

Since its founding for years ago, the Museum has held numerous exhibitions that have had a tremendous influence on all kinds of arts both within China and abroad. In addition to holding exhibitions of Chinese art within China, the Museum has held more than 100 exhibitions of works from abroad, such as the French 19th-century Village Views Painting Exhibition, the Boston Museum

The Oil Painting *Portrait of Qi Baishi* painted by Wu Zuoren.

of Fine Arts Famous American Painters' Original Works Exhibition, the Rodin Art Exhibit, the Famous Painters of Western Painting Exhibit, as well as many art exhibits with Australia, Japan, Russia, Germany, Korea, Malaysia, Norway and Israel.

Selected works of the National Art Museum of China have visited France, America, Japan, Russia, the Czech Republic, Turkey, Greece, and Korea, and have travelled many times to Hong Kong, Macao, and Taiwan.

National Museum of Modern Chinese Literature

Address: Beijing, Chaoyang District, Wenxueguan Road, #45
Website: www.wxg.org.cn

The National Museum of Modern Chinese Literature is located in the Chaoyang District of Beijing. The Museum constitutes the primary resource in China for materials on Chinese modern literature and it is also the largest building in the world dedicated solely to literature and to collections relating to literature. Resources include a library, a documents hall, a hall for research materials, and a center for academic exchange. The mission of the museum is to collect, conserve, organize, and research works of modern and contemporary authors of China, their manuscripts, translations, books and letters, diaries, recordings, videos, photographs, documents and any other materials that relate to the critique of a work such as literary journals and newspaper reviews.

The exterior of the National Museum of Modern Chinese Literature.

The Museum was established in March of 1985. Its collecting principles do not distinguish on the basis of political views, artistic school or sect or style. All new literary materials since the beginning of the 20th century can be collected, including works from Hong Kong, Macao and Taiwan, and also overseas Chinese-language works. The museum currently has more than 380,000 collected items, among them 230,000 books, 2,100 kinds of magazines, 142 kinds of newspapers, 13,824 handwritten manuscripts, 16,173 photographs, 11,600 letters, 360 taped recordings, 442 videos, and 4,380 cultural artifacts.

The Museum has set up special rooms or cases for whole collections that have been donated to the museum. It has also set up collections in the name of the person donating. Such cases include the special collections of Ba Jin (1904–2005), Bing Xin (1900–1999), Xia Yan (1900–1995) and some fifty more authors, including those

The statue of Bing Xin displayed in gardens of the National Museum of Modern Chinese Literature.

A portrait of Ba Jin collected by the National Museum of Modern Chinese Literature.

The garden in the National Museum of Modern Chinese Literature.

from Hong Kong, Taiwan and overseas such as Lin Haiyin (1918–2001), and Bu Shaofu (1909–2000).

The National Museum of Modern Chinese Literature actively carries on all kinds of literary activities, and has collectively edited a number of works on modern authors, as well as editing a quarterly journal together with the Modern Literature Research Association. Scholars both in China and abroad have carried on extensive interaction through the work of this museum. They have organized some major exhibits such as a retrospective of the works of Lao She (1899–1966), of Ye Shengtao (1894–1988), and a one-hundred-year tribute to Mao Dun (1896–1981).

The Museum has a multi-capacity hall that is offered for use as a site for literary discussions, research, speeches, performances, and exhibitions. A television hall is set up for televised events, and there is a media production room. The Museum is in a secluded garden full of trees. Inside, certain works of art were created specifically for the new museum by famous sculptors, painters, and craftsmen. There are oil paintings on the walls, colored glass inlaid in the walls, authors' sculptures, authors' signatures on ceramic vases and so on, providing an artistic atmosphere that is comfortable and conducive to reflection.

Beijing Theater Museum

Address: Beijing, Xuanwu District, Hufang Road, #3

Among the hundreds of *huiguan* (guildhall) houses built during the Ming and Qing dynasties, the one called Huguang Huiguan is best preserved of them all. It was originally built in 1807, in the twelfth year of the Jiaqing reign of the Qing dynasty. It is situated at the southwest corner of the intersection at Hufang Qiao. In 1997, it was completely renovated and reopened as what is now called the "Beijing Theater Museum."

The most valuable part of the complex is a theater building that was constructed in 1830. This is the most ancient of all of China's extant indoor theaters. The floor space of the first floor measures 568 square meters and the second floor is 328 meters, making a total of 896 square meters for the theater. The stage is 54 square meters. The main structural elements are the two great beams and nine crossbeams that span 11.36 meters, which is rare among buildings in China.

Today, eight-sided tables are placed around the lower level, and upstairs are boxes for seating; altogether the theater can hold an audience of 250. The ancient theater has been repainted but has not lost its refined elegance.

The old Xiangxianci building is currently the exhibition hall of the theater museum. It gives a brief history of the development of theater and in the process one can see that the institution of such a *huiguan*, or gathering spot, was very important for the development of Peking opera. In the Qing dynasty, when theaters from elsewhere came into Beijing they used the *huiguan* theaters for performances. The Anhui Huiguan would perform Hui-plays, the Huguang Huiguan would perform Chu-plays, the Jiangxi Huiguan would perform Gan-plays: this allowed all the different kinds of theater the opportunity to see each other and draw inspiration and lessons from each other. The exchange and blending finally created the conditions for the birth of the ultimate Chinese theater, Peking opera. Some of the masterpieces of the theater were first performed in the Anhui Huiguan, such as Peach-blossom Fan. Great masters of the stage such as Master Tan Xinpei (1846–1943), Mei Lanfang (1894–1961) and others have all in the past performed here. Historical treasures relating to the theater are stored in the Xiangxianci part of the Wenchang pavilion. There are, for instance, the costumes worn by Yang Xiaolou (1879–1938), there are early period records made by the EMI Company, and so on.

The main gate of the Beijing Theater Museum set up in Huguang Guildhall.

China Sports Museum

Address: Beijing City, Anding Men Wai, Anding Road, #3A
Website: www.bjkp.gov.cn/kpcg/kpcg/bowuguan/newpage225.htm

The China Sports Museum is located in Beijing on the southeast side of the Olympic Center outside Anding Men. The building is quite extraordinary. It opens out like an octagonal fan, or like a whirlwind that is about to take off, symbolizing the powerful development of Chinese sports.

The China Sports Museum is the first specialized museum devoted to collecting, exhibiting, and researching sports culture and sports-culture history. It covers 7,200 square meters, including an exhibition area of 2,510 square meters. It holds five exhibition halls altogether, one central hall and four that exhibit various types of objects. A large stone-carved statue of a dragon boat greets the visitor in the main foyer. Dragon-boat racing is the quintessential traditional Chinese sport and therefore this fine, inlaid version of a dragon boat is appropriate.

The first hall holds the ancient Chinese sports section. This has a strong ethnic flavor: dragons coil up the golden pillars, palace lanterns are hung high above, everything feels ancient. The exhibition moves chronologically from pre-Qin, to

The exterior of the China Sports Museum.

The Song dynasty "One Hundred Play" carved on stones.

Han and Three Kingdoms, Westerm and Easterm Jin, North and South dynasties, then Sui, Tang and Five dynasties, Song, Liao, Jin, Yuan, Ming and Qing. All reflect the accomplishments of China's ancient sports development. Items displayed include photographs, pictures, rubbings, documents and historical material, and such archaeological works as the Tang dynasty polo players.

The second hall is for China's modern sports from 1840 up to the year 1949, explaining the changes in this period through the use of historical photographs and actual objects. For example, the earliest China football team cards, dating from 1902, are displayed; there is a special edition of a 1904 sports magazine, photographs of China's participation in the first Far East Sports Rally, the 1936 Berlin Olympics, and so on.

The third, fourth and fifth halls exhibit the sports accomplishments of the People's Republic of China. Using more than 500 objects and more than 500 photographs, this portrays the support of the party and the government for sports enterprises. It includes competitive sports as well as general recreation sports, and covers sports arena design, sports psychology, and so on, all of these reflecting the past sixty years of Chinese sports accomplishments. The sixth hall uses more than 300 photographs and around 500 objects to display special qualities of China's various regions and 56 nationalities. It portrays local traditional sports in particular.

Hong Kong Museum of History

Address: Hong Kong Special Administrative Region, Kowloon, Tsimshatsui,
Chatham Road South, #100
Website: www.lcsd.gov.hk/CE/Museum/History

The Hong Kong Museum of History was formerly called the Hong Kong Museum. The new museum was opened to the public in 1998; it is located in Tsimshatsui, Kowloon. The permanent exhibition of this museum shows "The Story of Hong Kong," which portrays in a lively way the natural ecology, local customs, historical developments and traditional culture.

The Museum currently has over 90,000 objects in its collections, which are divided into archaeological, local history, people's history, and natural history. Among the archaeological objects are items discovered on China's southeastern shore, and articles exca-

Hong Kong Museum of History.

An old gramophone collected by the Hong Kong Museum of History.

vated in the 1930s in the southern islands.

Archival photographs are an important historical resource and the Museum collection is rich in these, with the earliest dating back to the 1860s. Other objects in the collection include models of town and village architecture, early newspapers and documents, a complete set of Hong Kong money, and family genealogies from an old town in the New Territories.

Collections relating to people's customs include fishing equipment and models of fishing ships, traditional clothes, village furniture and daily articles, items relating to local customs and beliefs, dolls, entertainment items and so on. The natural history collections include shells of sea animals, butterflies, and all kinds of gems and minerals.

The Hong Kong Museum of History has held more than 60 thematic exhibitions since its establishment, such as Fifty years of Hong

A corner of the interior display of the Hong Kong Museum of History—models of Fujian sea boat and painted trade boat.

Kong archaeology, Living history: protecting the historical architecture of Hong Kong, Hong Kong money, Hong Kong historical materials, Hong Kong postage stamps over 150 years, and so on. These exhibitions have wide-ranging subject matter. They delve deeply into Hong Kong

The night scene of Hong Kong.

history from various perspectives, and they have been helpful in enhancing cultural exchange between Hong Kong and neighboring regions.

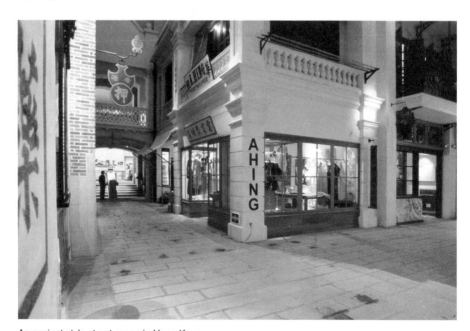

An ancient style street scene in Hong Kong.

Macao Maritime Museum

Address: Macao, Largo do Pagode da Barra, #1
Website: www.museumaritimo.gov.mo

The Macao Maritime Museum is located near the Mage Temple on Mage Street in Macao. It was established and opened to the public in 1990 and is a specialized museum focusing on maritime relations. It is under the jurisdiction of the Macao Port Office.

The Maritime Museum "was built for the mariners' friends of all the world's peoples." The building is a completely enclosed construction of three levels. It is located on the southwest end of the Macao peninsula, next to the harbour. Nearby is the #1 wharf where a Huating and a dragon boat are docked, which are also for visitors' enjoyment.

The Museum currently has around 2,000 objects in its collection. These introduce the boats in which Portuguese came to Macao in

The underground exhibition area—maritime folk custom.

The exterior of Macao Maritime Museum.

the early period, as well as traditional Chinese ships and equipment. Included are also navigation tools used in Macao today. Exhibitions are divided into the fishing industry, Portuguese and Chinese discoveries, technology, and transport.

The exhibition area in the 2nd floor—Maritime history.

The fishing section introduces fishing equipment and fish-cultivation technology. Models of boats, nets, ways to catch fish and some scenes of fishermen actually catching fish are shown. The section on Portuguese and Chinese discoveries shows how the Portuguese Vasco da Gama led a fleet to this area in the late 15th century, how he discovered the passage to India and how other Portuguese explorers came to the Malaysian archipelago and on to China and Japan. The

The exhibition area in the 3rd floor—Navigation technology.

early period of China's maritime industry is also described, with the history of Zheng He heading out on the western seas in the early 15th century.

The Museum also exhibits a large number of military weapons and devices used on the high seas, such as guns, cannons, telescopes and so on, showing the importance of the defense of trade routes.

Gardens and Architectural Monuments

China has long been renowned as a birthplace of gardens. The grounds and buildings of ancient Far Eastern gardens are masterpieces of the art of merging man and nature in a harmonious whole. They also unify art and technology.

Suzhou Garden Museum

Address: Jiangsu Province, Suzhou City, Pingjiang District, Dongbei Street,
#202
Website: www.szgarden.sz.js.cn

Suzhou is known as a Garden City. As the saying goes, "The gardens south of the river are first under heaven, while those of Suzhou are the crowning achievement of those south of the river." These exquisite gardens are the ultimate expression of China's ancient architecture and arts, and they are the distillation of the cultural history of the famous city of Suzhou.

The marvelous quality of Suzhou's gardens lies in the fact that they use a tiny amount of land to realize the creative abilities of the craftsman. The twists and turns allow a new view at every step and allow the revelation of microcosms of gardens within gardens and macrocosms of views outside of views. When you walk into a garden you suddenly put yourself in a painting. Among the many gardens, four have been declared the masterpieces: these are the Canglang Pavilion of the Song dynasty,

The Lion Forest.

Zhuozheng Garden.

the Lion Forest of the Yuan dynasty, the Zhuozheng Garden of the Ming dynasty, and the Liu Yuan of the Qing dynasty. These represent the artistic styles of their respective dynasties.

In order to commemorate the 2,500[th] anniversary year of Suzhou, a Gardens Museum was established inside the Zhuozheng Garden in 1992. In 2007, the new hall of the Museum was opened to the public. The new hall is situated on Dongbei Road. It covers 4,000 square meters of ground and includes 3,390 square meters of building structure. It adjoins the Zhuozheng Garden and the Taipingtianguo Loyal King's residence. Both new and old halls are in use at the present time.

Inside the old hall, the exhibitions mainly introduce the history of Suzhou's ancient gardens, in addition to their current status and the artistry of garden design. Four halls cover various aspects of the subject. The first describes the objective reasons for basing such superlative gardens in Suzhou: the preconditions, including mountains and rivers, the ancient history, the flourishing economy, the confluence of peoples and the many generations of skilled artisans.

The second describes the history of the gardens. This gives a comprehensive overview of their development and progress. The gardens began in the Spring and Autumn periods of the Zhou dynasty, long before China was unified in 221 BC. By the time of the Wei, Jin and the North and South dynasties, temples and private families were creating different kinds of gardens. In the Song and Yuan dynasties, piled up rocks became the rage, in the Ming and Qing eras garden pavilions flourished.

The third hall introduces the contours and styles of Suzhou's ancient gardens as they are today, as well as the international influence of these gardens.

The fourth introduces garden construction. This reflects the many-layered approach of Suzhou's gardens, the layering of mountains, water, buildings, flowers, trees. All are blended together to form the four great traits of a garden. Traditional artistic constraints are used to create both poetic meaning and visual results.

The main displays in this museum are models that show arrangements of gardens, especially those that no longer exist. There are twenty-four such

The Lingering Garden in Suzhou.

displays, including Suzhou-style gardens built abroad and other famous gardens of the South. Zhuozheng Garden is an example of gardens within the museum; it uses miniature mountains and rock crags to create its illusions. A number of other gardens use water as their main component. Both the gardens themselves and the museum are well worth visiting.

Summer Palace

Address: Beijing City, Haidian District, Xinjian Gongmen Road, #19
Website: www.yiheyuan.com

The Summer Palace, located in the western suburbs of Beijing, is the last imperial garden built by the feudal dynasties of ancient China. It was destroyed by the British and French Allied Armies in 1860; the Empress Dowager Cixi (1835–1908) then appropriated the navy's budget to rebuild it. In 1998, this imperial garden, which belongs to world civilization, was entered in the ranks of World Cultural Heritage.

Entering the garden from the East Palace gate, one first passes through an impressive gate and comes upon seven halls that are situated facing eastward. These are the "Morally Upright" halls

The Yulan Hall in the Summer Palace where Emperor Guangxu read and called in subordinates.

Wax statues of "An eunuch combing hair for Cixi" displayed in the Summer Palace.

where the Qing emperors met with various ministers. Inside are preserved the thrones used by the Empress Dowager and the last Emperor Guangxu while they were on the throne. Also on display are various paraphernalia of the time including incense burners of bronze dragon and phoenix, candlesticks, the mythical beast called the "chilin,"and the screen

that is so pervasive a part of Chinese culture.

Passing further westward, one soon comes to the lake, and to a hall, Yulan Tang, that was built for the relaxation of the Emperor Qianlong. This was rebuilt in the 18th year of Guangxu and made into a sleeping chamber for the Guangxu Emperor. In 1898, after Cixi put the Reform Movement into motion, she locked Guangxu up inside this small palace. She had the corridors to east, west and north all sealed or blocked up with brick

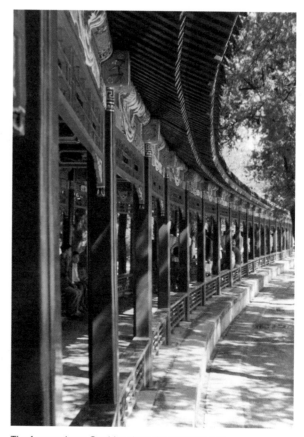

The famous Long Corridor along the Kunming Lake.

The Buddhist Incense Pavilion.

The Marble Boat.

walls, while the southern entryway was watched day and night by a eunuch that she personally trusted.

The Leshou Tang Main Hall was the resting palace of Cixi. To the left and right on the stairs are around six different kinds of bronze deer, cranes, and vases, that signify peaceful togetherness. The suite to the west was Cixi's bedroom. The rooms to the east were for changing clothes. Subsidiary halls to east and west were stations for female officials and palace women who were on duty.

On the northern bank of the Kunming Lake is a long corridor, also called the thousand-steps corridor, that is world-famous for its fine craftsmanship. It contains 273 small "rooms" and is 728 meters in length—the longest corridor in any form of Chinese garden or ancient architecture. The four octagonal pavilions that are spaced along it, for stopping and resting, have ornate descriptive names and symbolize the four seasons. Some 8, 000 paintings are painted directly on the beams of the corridor. They narrate stories of famous people in Chinese history and portray decorative scenes.

The central axis of the entire garden is formed by drawing an imaginary line from the central ridge of the backdrop of the Wanshou Mountain, from to the Buddhist Incense Pavilion. A hall called the Parting the Clouds Hall graces the mountain ridge and is considered the most beautiful of the entire garden. It can be reached by ascending a set of stairs and will reward the visitor with lovely sights. To the north of the hall stands the south-central ridge of the Wanshou Mountain, and on that stands the central building of the Summer Palace, the Buddha Incense pavilion. Three Buddha statues are inside the Pavilion, which stands an impressive 41 meters tall.

To the western end of the long corridor, beside the lake, is the only structure in the Summer Palace that has a western character. This is a stone boat that is 36 meters long. The cabin on it is made of wood, and it is furnished with western-style tables and chairs. A number of other locations in the Summer Palace are of both historical and aesthetic interest, with the so-called Eight Views of Hui Mountain being among them. When the Qianlong Emperor took his famous southern tour, he viewed an ancient garden in the town of Wuxi and resolved to build a replica of it on his return to the north. This became the Huishan Bajing, the Eight Views of Huishan at the Summer Palace.

The Summer Palace was invaded and destroyed first by the English and French Allied Army and then again by the Eight-Powers

The night scene of Suzhou Street.

The big stage in Dehe Garden.

United Army. It underwent extensive restoration and was reopened in various stages, starting in 1986. In 1992, other buildings were reconstructed on their original sites; in 2003 Qianlong's garden plans were basically restored. This outstanding Chinese Imperial Garden Museum is famous worldwide not only for its construction and views but also for its rich collection of art. More than 40,000 items are in the collection, among which 93 are regarded as extremely rare treasures of "national-level" status.

Great Wall Museum of China

Address: Beijing, Yanqing County, Badaling scenic district
Website: www.cnwh.org/cnsites/nwlcc/wlcc.htm

Coming to China and not visiting the Great Wall is like going to Egypt and neglecting the pyramids. It is the equivalent of not really visiting the ancient civilization. One of the architectural wonders of the world, the scope of the Great Wall dates from when the Qin dynasty unified China. It reaches a hypothetical "ten thousand *li*" from east to west: its name in Chinese literally means the ten-thousand-*li* Long Wall.

This term is descriptive: a *li* is roughly one-third of a mile and ten-thousand *li* signifies a very long distance. Different parts of the Wall were constructed through the many dynasties of Chinese history, over the course of more than two thousand years. In extent, though not in one connected line, the different parts of the Wall stretch from the portal known as Jiayuguan in Gansu in the west all the way to the pass called Shanhaiguan in Hebei in the east. During the Ming dynasty many parts of the wall were rebuilt using stone blocks and earthen bricks that had been used

The majestic appearance of the Beijing Badaling Great Wall.

The autumn scene of the Beijing Badaling Great Wall.

before. The resulting Wall represents much of what can be seen today.

The Great Wall in the vicinity of Beijing's "Badaling Pass" is the best part of the Ming-dynasty reconstructed wall. This section uses stones as the foundation and pounded-earth as the core, and is faced with a special kind of brick. Its average height is 7.8 meters and average breadth is 6.5 meters: it could accommodate five or six horses riding abreast along the top. At intervals along the wall are towers for both surveillance and for shooting; also fire towers that were used to transmit military information. Portals allow passage at certain intervals: the great portal outside Beijing is known as Juyongguan.

The Jiayuguan Pass in Gansu Province.

In 1994, a "Great Wall Museum of China" was built on the western side of the Badaling Pass. Its exhibition hall covers 3,200 square meters and is divided into several exhibition rooms. The permanent exhibition is composed of eight different parts: the historical Great Wall, the Ming-dynasty Great Wall, the building and fortifications, the Great Wall's military and political significance, economic and cultural exchange along the Great Wall, arts of national minorities, literature and arts, Love My China Repair My Great Wall, the First among Famous Places, and Rainbow of Friendship. Exhibitions in these various sections display all kinds of historical objects and show functions of the Wall that included both peaceful economic exchange and protective military power.

The tablet erected when the Huangyaguan Great Wall was built in the Ming dynasty.

In addition to the locations for viewing the Great Wall north of Beijing, many other parts of the Wall can be visited as well. The portal in the far west, called Jiayuguan, is known as the "greatest pass under heaven" and is well worth visiting. The one in the east, at Shanhaiguan or "Mountain-Ocean-Pass," is of tremendous significance in Chinese history. All of these are open to visitors and have historical objects on display.

The Mutianyu Great Wall.

Temple of Heaven

Address: Beijing, Chongwen District, Tiantan Road
Webpage: www.tiantanpark.com

The Temple of Heaven is located in the southeastern part of modern-day Beijing, on the east side of Yongdingmennei Street. It once lay outside the ancient city precinct and was the site of imperial offerings to heaven during the Ming and Qing dynasties. Over the course of thousands of years of imperial offerings in China, it is the only one of such sites remaining today. A group of buildings, gardens, and surrounding groves, it is highly symbolic and is a museum of a very special nature. The State Council has declared it to be a key cultural protected unit and in 1998 it was listed by UNESCO as a World Cultural Heritage Site.

Construction of the Temple of Heaven was begun in 1420, during the Ming dynasty under the Emperor Yongle. After Yongle had

A heaven sacrificing and harvest praying ritual performance held in the Qinian Hall in the Temple of Heaven.

The Yuanqiu Altar in the Temple of Heaven in Beijing.

settled on Beijing as the site of the capital, the buildings and surrounding areas were later rebuilt and enlarged during the reigns of Jiajing of the Ming and Qianlong of the Qing.

The general layout of the Temple of Heaven incorporates the ancient Chinese configuration of a "round heaven and a square earth." This symbolic form ties in to a north-south geographic alignment, with the concept of "north-round-south-square." Two layers of walls surround the temple precincts. The outer wall's circumference is 6,553 meters with a space inside of 270,000 square meters, which is about four times the size of Beijing's Palace Museum. The site once occupied a large percentage of what was the outskirts of ancient Beijing.

The Qigu Altar and the Qinian Hall

These two are located in the northern part of the Tiantan complex. They comprise a large and imposing set of buildings and are the most representative architecture of the Temple of Heaven. The lower part of the Qinian Hall is a three-tiered white marble round platform, surrounded by a stone railing. The upper part is a round-shaped hall that is built without cross beams. Its ceiling is arched and pointed and its roof is covered with blue glazed tiles. The cir-

The Imperial Vault of Heaven in the Temple of Heaven.

cumference of the lower tier of the platform is 90.8 meters and its total height is 5.56 meters. The Hall is located in its very center, and has a diameter of 32.72 meters and a height of 38 meters. The top part of the Hall holds a round-shaped *baoding* or topknot that is gilded. Twenty-eight cypress (*nanmu*) pillars are arrayed around the Hall. Inside the hall, stand four dragon-well pillars with diameter of 1.2 meters, and height of 19.2 meters. The ambiance of this hall is enhanced by the way the ceiling rises towards the sky. On the northern side inside the hall is a dragon-carved throne on a supporting dais, and a stele to the ancestors and gods of the emperors. On a special day of the first month of every year, the emperor would lead his princes and officials here to pray for good harvests, and, if they were encountering drought, they would come here to pray for rain.

On the various sides of the Qinian Hall are subsidiary buildings that were used for various imperial purposes. Altogether they form a harmonious group.

The Yuanqiu Altar and Imperial Vault of Heaven

This altar is not as grand as that in the Qinian Hall but is still a very important part of the Tiantan, for this is where the emperor made sacrifices to heaven. The altar was built in the 9th year of Jiaqing, or 1530. It was originally covered in blue-glazed tiles. In the 14th year of Qianlong (1749) it was expanded and was faced with marble, taking on its current aspect. The altar is round and divided into three levels, each with nine stairs leading up it on each of the four cardinal directions. In the center of the top level is a round central stone, with nine circles of stones arrayed around it. Each level has numerous indicators of nine or of multiples of nine. The craftsmen took pains to emphasize this number, since it was seen as an indicator of "yang" or the male principle, and this in turn was seen as a confirmation of the intent of heaven.

Behind the circular altar lie a group of buildings including a round structure called the Emperor's mystic realm or Vault of Heaven. These buildings were begun in the 9th year of Jiajing (1631). They were repaired in the 8th year of Qianlong (1743). They include a circular hall with pointed roofline, inside which the ceiling extends upward in layers. A carved stone base holds a stelae that celebrates the emperor. The thing that most attracts people's attention at this place is the "echo" wall that surrounds it as well as the so-called triple-sound stones.

In addition to the temples and altars comprising the main architecture of the Tiantan, a number of subsidiary buildings exist that were used for operational purposes. These included rooms for cooking, preparing the sacrifices, and storing things. A building called the Zhaigong is where the emperor would sleep before making the sacrifices and praying to the gods of harvest. Another site of interest is believed to be one of the earliest groups of buildings at the Tiantan. It was built in the 18th year of Ming-dynasty Yongle (1420), and was specifically made for music to accompany the sacrifices. It served as a practice room for the music masters, and was also used for storing the instruments. From this, we can understand how important music was as an integral part of the imperial rites.

Temple and Cemetery of Confucius and the Kong Family Mansion in Qufu

Address: Shandong Province, Qufu City
Website: www.cnwh.org/cnsites/nsk/kmklkf.htm

Qufu, in Shandong Province, was the capital of the ancient State of Lu, dating back some 3,000 years ago. It is regarded as one of the famous historical cities in Chinese history, and it is also the homeland of the late Spring and Autumn-period philosopher and educator known as Confucius. In Chinese, this man is known as Kongzi; he was a historical person who lived from 551 to 479 BC. The passage of history has layered Qufu with many cultural traces—among the most notable of these are the Confucius Temple, family mansion, and cemetery, which occupy the smaller half of the town.

Confucius Temple

The entryway to this temple passes through a precinct that is

Confucius sacrificing ritual performance held in the Dacheng Hall in the Confucius Temple in Qufu.

The dragon pillars of the Dacheng Hall in the Confucius Temple.

dotted with ancient trees and that leads the visitor through a passageway of cypresses. The entry is from the south, through the southern gate of the ancient town. A forest of stone stelae testifies to the long history of the place, which measures some 327 mu in size and is more than one kilometer in length from north to south.

The main building of the Confucius Temple is called the Dacheng Hall. It is a magnificent building enhanced with 28 coiled dragon pillars and vermilion and golden tiles. Successive generations conducted rituals here in honor of Confucius. Rituals began in the second year after Confucius died, namely in 478 BC, when Lu Aigong turned Confucius' home into a temple. Since that time, dynasty after dynasty of emperors have remodeled and renovated the place, till it has arrived at its current state. The buildings of the temple copy the layout and style of imperial palaces, with nine courtyards and a central axis that runs north-south. There are some 466 rooms in the Confucius temple, with numerous halls and pavilions, in addition to 55 gate buildings.

The Kong Family Mansion

To the east of the Confucius Temple is the family mansion. It has been the site of official offices as well as the private home of many

The main gate of the Confucius Residence ñ the Lingxing Gate.

generations of the Sage. Its former name was Yansheng Gong residence; Yansheng Gong was a descendant in the direct line of descent from Confucius. The residence covers an area of more than 240 *mu* and includes 463 halls and rooms. It has nine courtyards divided by three passageways: the eastern passageway is where the family shrine is located. The western passageway contains the study of the Sage, where he read books and studied poetry and the rites.

The main part of the family mansion is located along the middle passageway. Before this

The residence of Kong Lingyi—the 76th generation of Confucius.

are situated a number of palace administrative offices. The rear part is the residence, and at the very rear is the garden, which is called "Iron Mountain Garden." A large number of works of art are preserved in the family seat, the most famous of which are ten Shang and Zhou-dynasty bronze vessels for offerings. With their elegant forms, exquisite ornamentation, and clear inscriptions, these are considered some of China's rarest treasures. One of the fine paintings in the collection is of the Three Sages by the Yuan-dynasty painter and calligrapher Zhao Mengfu. A copy of a portion of the *Confucian Analects* is on display that is written in such small script that one can read it only by using a magnifying glass. Even more valuable are the nearly ten thousand scrolls and documents from the Ming and Qing dynasties. From many different perspectives, these reflect the political, economic, philosophical and cultural aspects of ancient China.

Confucius Cemetery

One arrives at the famed Confucius woods (cemetery) after leaving Qufu by exiting through the northern gate and passing through the row of cypress trees and exquisitely carved stone stelae. The woods occupy 3,000 *mu* of land and are where Confucius and his descendants are buried. This area represents the best-preserved and most complete set of ancestral clan tombs in China. Going through the Sage Woods Gate, one arrives at an arboretum that was planted, tree by tree, by the many generations of disciples of Confucius.

The Confucius Tomb in Confucius Woods.

Jinci Museum

Address: Shanxi Province, Taiyuan City, Jinci Town
Website: www.chinajinci.com

The Jin Ancestral Hall (Jinci) is located in Taiyuan City of Shanxi Province, 25 kilometers to the south of the city, at the foot of a mountain. This is the oldest architectural monument remaining in China that has confirmable historical documentation. It also has the oldest garden, and is hallowed ground that melds natural scenery with an ancient human presence.

The Jin Ancestral Hall is located at the source of the Jin River. It was officially dedicated to Tangshu Yu, a younger brother of King of Zhou, who lived in the 11th century BC. Because of its location on the Jin River, Yu changed the name of his state to Jin, and in paying respects to Yu life, later generations named the place the Jin Ancestral Hall. Although the buildings have been renovated and expanded many times, the original site has not changed. In the years 1023–1032, during the Northern Song dynasty, an additional Sacred Mother Temple was built and the An-

An iron man of the Song dynasty in the Jinci Museum.

The Naolaoquan Pavilion in the Jinci Museum.

cestral Hall was substantially enlarged. In 1168, during the Jin dynasty, another commemorative hall and other buildings were added, until it gradually came to assume the shape and size that it is today.

The Jinci Museum includes the original buildings of the place, the gardens, and woods, the spring, the sculpture, and the carved stelae. Key items on exhibit include, most importantly, the Sacred Mother Temple. This is one of the earliest remaining large-scale wooden buildings in the world, with unique spatial arrangement, internal structure, and artistic form. There are 43 Northern Song-period painted statues inside the hall, treasures among painted clay sculpture in China. The main statue is of the Sacred Mother, who sits in a wooden case in the middle of the Hall. The other 42 are arrayed on either side as well as around the perimeter of the Hall.

A great flying beam bridge is set across the square-shaped fish pond in front of the Sacred Mother Hall. This bridge was built in the Tiansheng period of the Northern Song and is built in the shape of a cross. It sits on 34 small octagonal stone pillars that are set in the water on stone-carved lotus blossoms. A *dougong* construction is set on the pillars, with traditional-Chinese crossbeams and blocks. On these are set the beams and the planks of the bridge. The surface of the bridge is covered with bricks, and stone railings line on either side. On the moon platform on the eastern side of the bridge is a pair of iron lions that were cast in the 8th year of Zhenghe, or in 1118.

Another of the great treasures in this place is an inscribed stele erected in the Baohan Pavilion. This stands 195 cm in height, is 127 cm wide and 27 cm thick, and holds an inscription that was

The flying beam bridge in the Jinci Museum.

written by the Tang emperor, Tang Taizong. It is composed of 203 characters and is written in cursive script.

The spring that is the source of the Jin River is the primary reason the Ancestral Hall is located in this place. This spring is clear and pure and runs year-round at a constant temperature of 17 degrees centigrade. It waters a number of trees in the vicinity, one of which is an ancient cypress that is said to be 3,000 years old. The flow rate of the spring is 1.8 cubic meters per second: this emerges from a pavilion that stands over the actual source, and then is channeled into north and south canals.

The ancient buildings of the Ancestral Hall also hold a collection of valuable artifacts. In addition to the Hall, other ancient architectural monuments include an Ancestral Hall to Tangshu Yu, a water-reflecting pavilion, a golden-man platform, a clock and drum tower, and a sacred long-life temple. A library also enriches the substantial holdings of this ancient place.

Lady-maid statues of the Song dynasty in the Sacred Mother Hall in the Jinci Museum.

Homes of Our Forebears:
Archaeology

The vast lands of the cultural continuum that has come to be called China are one of the cradles of early man. From Paleolithic to Neolithic periods, early people have left their advancing footprints on this land.

Zhoukoudian Peking Man Site Museum

Address: Beijing City, Fangshan District, Zhoukoudian Xiang
Website: www.zkd.cn

The site of this historic archaeological discovery, set on a low hill called Dragon-Bone Mountain at Zhoukoudian, 50 kilometers to the southwest of Beijing, marks one of the origins of early man. The resulting finds became known to the world as "Peking Man" or Beijing Man. Because of this, the site was declared an important National Cultural Protected Unit in 1961, and was listed as one of UNESCO's World Cultural Heritage Sites in 1987.

Autumn is the most congenial season in Beijing, and is also best at Dragon-Bone Mountain. The reconstructed dioramas at the exhibition hall of early man that describe a period some 400–500,000 years ago are also set in the fall. Peking Man utilized the southward migration of deer and other animals to surround and hunt

The exterior of the Zhoukoudian Peking Man Site Museum.

The restored head statue of the Peking Man.

these tasty wild creatures. Women and children plucked ripe berries and fruit in this season, and also gathered grains in preparation for the cold winter.

The site of Zhoukoudian is set into a mountainside, with running water available nearby. Natural caves existed in these mountains and the weather was warmer long ago. The natural environment was conducive to habitation and Peking Man is believed to have lived here continuously for some 300,000 years. Evidence of this habitation has been left behind in the caves, in the forms of bones, worked stones, and traces of occupation.

The main cave measures 140 meters from east to west and 53 meters from north to south. At twilight on a cold early winter's evening in 1929, with the help of a lighted candle, archaeologists crawled into the space of this cave and found the extraordinary discovery of a complete early hominid cranium from 500,000 years ago. The name given to it was China Primitive Man, Peking-type. Or, in short, Peking Man.

Peking Man left several tens of thousands of Paleolithic stone tools behind him in this and neighboring caves, made in many shapes and from many types of stone. These can be seen in the exhibition cases of the museum. Through long periods of experimentation, Peking Man became familiar with the different uses and chipping qualities of different

The Peking Man Crania found in the Peking Man Site in Zhoukoudian.

kinds of stone. Peking Man's use of fire deserves special mention: these people were in possession of the knowledge of how use fire to cook food, stay warm, give light, and keep off wild animals. The use of fire delin-

The restored image of Peking Men going hunting.

eated an epoch-making chapter in the history of man's advancement.

In 1973, the so-called "New Cave Man" was discovered at Zhoukoudian, representing a stage in man's history of advancement to "early hominids," dating to 200,000 to 100,000 years ago. Around 20,000 years ago, the humans living in the vicinity of Zhoukoudian were given the name Mountaintop Cave Man following their discovery in a cave above the Peking Man Cave. This earlier discovery was made in 1933, and indicated that the inhabitants had already entered a matrilineal-clan commune stage. The most representative works of the Mountaintop Cave Man were an 82-millimeter bone needle, its surface still shiny and slightly arced in shape, with one side still very sharp. On the other end some very fine instrument had hollowed out a tiny hole. The appearance of this object proved that the Mountaintop Cave Man already sewed and clothed himself with animal hides and leather. A number of interesting ornaments were excavated from the site, including earrings, animal teeth with holes in them for stringing, fishbones, ocean shells, stone beads, bones carved in certain ways, and so on. This indicated that people of the time had an appreciation of aesthetics and of how to adorn themselves.

Shenyang Xinle Site Museum

Address: Liaoning Province, Shenyang City, Longshan Road, #1
Website: www.lnwh.gov.cn/bwg1/xl.htm

The Shenyang Xinle Site Museum is located in the northern part of the Huanggu District of Shenyang City, Liaoning Province. It is divided into northern and southern components: the southern has an exhibition hall for displaying cultural relics, while the northern is the actual archaeological site and is an important protected cultural property. The northern section covers an area of 22,500 square meters and preserves a large-scale primitive dwelling site by reproducing in open-air form ten dwellings from the Neolithic period, together with a simulated lifestyle of people living at that time. Together, the two areas total 52,500 square meters.

The discovery of this Neolithic site was first made at the Xinle Electric Power Plant, hence the name. The excavations are divided into Upper Strata and Lower Strata cultures, with the Upper Strata belonging to a period roughly 3,000 years ago. This corresponds

The exterior of the Shenyang Xinle Site Museum.

with the bronze period, and excavated objects include ceramics such as three-legged vessels and stone tools that are predominantly of the polished-tool type. The Lower Strata belongs to a period

The wood carving Sun Bird.

roughly 7,200 years ago, or what is considered to be a primitive-society Neolithic period. Half-submerged or half-underground dwellings reveal the contemporary architecture. Recovered artifacts include deep-bellied pots with impressed rope patterns, microliths, polished stone tools, chipped stone tools, carbonized particles, and wooden carved items. Since this culture had unique characteristics and was important in researching the history of early peoples in the northeast, it was given the name Xinle Culture.

After repeated excavations, the Xinle site has produced around thirty habitations in the Lower Strata Xinle Culture. Larger buildings are around 120 square meters in area, medium-sized are around 40–60 square meters, and small-sized are around 20–30 square meters. These are spaced closely together in lines so that this is considered to be a Neolithic settlement.

The Xinle Site Museum in the southern district currently has around 1,200 objects in its collection. In the northern district of the museum, one half-underground house has been preserved and is on view in its original state. This homesite was excavated in 1978. It is rectangular in shape, covers 95.46 square meters, and there is a round hearth in the middle. The four walls of the pit show the remaining traces of columns. A large number of items were excavated from within the house that are now exhibited mostly in the form in which archaeologists found them at the time. This, together with the actual structure of a dwelling that people used 7,000 years ago, gives visitors an authentic sense of what it was like to live here at that time.

Hemudu Site Museum

Address: Zhejiang Province, Yuyao City, Hemudu Town

Webite: www.hemudusite.com

The Hemudu Site Museum is located in Hemudu Town, Yuyao City, Zhejiang Province. The site dates from the early Neolithic period in southern China. It covers forty thousand square meters and has a cultural layer that is a total of 3.7 meters in depth. Four separate cultural layers can be distinguished that, after calibrated carbon fourteen testing, date to between 7,000 and 3,500 years ago. In 1982, this site was declared a National Key Cultural Protected Unit.

A bone spade-like plough unearthed in Hemudu.

The Hemudu Site Museum was opened in May of 1993 and is divided into two parts: the actual site of excavation and an exhibition of objects. It covers a total of 26,000

The exterior of the Hemudu Site Museum.

The original state of the Hemudu Site.

square meters and the building area covers a space of 3,163 square meters. The building area is composed of six separate buildings that are joined to one another by corridors. The general layout of the buildings conforms to the unique Hemudu style of architecture, which in Chinese is called ganlan-style, or trunk and railing. This includes a long ridgepole, short eaves, and a high foundation. The building rests on 456 pillars on which lie groups of cross beams, symbolizing the tenon and mortise technology already used some 7,000 years ago. The foyer is in the shape of a legendary "roc" spreading its wings, expressing the worship of birds that was practiced by the early Hemudu people.

This museum exhibits around 320 objects that were retrieved in two main excavation periods at the site. Among the objects are remains of rice kernels planted by man, ceramic fragments that have traces of carbonized rice grains, rice-husk-patterned pottery fragments, bone items, wooden joint pieces, ivory bird-shaped artefacts, ivory carved plate-shaped containers with sun motifs, jade items, and so on. These are all worthy of being described as

The restored external appearance of the hemudu Human residence.

gems of Neolithic culture.

The exhibition is divided into two parts, the permanent exhibition and the specimens exhibition. The permanent exhibition has three halls. The first covers 400 square meters and explains the basic situation of the 7,000-year-old site in terms of charts and photographs. The second hall covers 300 square meters, and reflects the hunting and gathering life as well as the rice-agriculture of the time. It exhibits actual items such as man-cultivated grain, agricultural implements made of bone, a husker made of wood, and stone grinders, ceramic axes, etc., as well as containers for holding food, appropriate for an exhibition of rice-producing culture. The third hall covers 400 square meters and includes two parts, one on the life of the settlement and one on its spiritual or intellectual culture. Exhibited here are pillars, beams, boards and other wooden architectural elements, wooden tools, stone ax, stone awl, bone awl, a reconstructed trunk and railing style building (portion), and a model of a well. Parts of a primitive loom are also displayed, including many things that no longer have contemporary names.

Xi'an Banpo Museum

Address: Shaanxi Province, Xi'an City, Banpo Road, #155
Webite: www.bpmuseum.com

The Xi'an Banpo Museum is located in a modern building some three miles to the east of Xi'an City in Shaanxi Province. It is near the bridge that crosses the Chan River, long renowned as one of the famous eight rivers of Chang'an. The Museum was built in 1958 and is the first museum built for a "prehistory site," a habitation site of early man. Its name comes from its location on the northern side of Banpo Village. The site marks a settlement that dates to the matrilineal clan commune period of the Neolithic period. Before its discovery in the twentieth century, it had been lying in wait for some 6,000 years.

The arrangement of the Neolithic village was quite organized. At the center of the settlement was a 160-square meter-large room that was surrounded by many smaller rooms. All of the doors of these faced the inside larger room, reflecting the clan spirit of a cohesive group. Around the village was a 300-meter long trench or ditch that was used to keep wild animals from attacking. To the east was a ceramic-making area and to the north was the cemetery

The exterior of the Xi'an Banpo Museum.

A basin of human face and fish pattern unearthed in Banpo.

A bottle with sharp-pointed bottom unearthed in Banpo.

district. Inside the town were some 46 houses. Some were square, some round, some half-submerged in the ground, some on the surface. These houses already used traditional Chinese wall-construction methods and can be called precursors of later Chinese architecture that used wood and earth.

In a reconstruction of a Banpo room are exhibited production tools and daily utensils that were used by Banpo people. On the walls are hung animal skins and pointed-bottom vessels for getting water. A mat is spread beside the hearth on the floor —the scene of ancient man's life is suddenly spread before our eyes: members of the clan, under the direction of the old grandmother, are just in the process of making a fire. Or outside, hunters are taking aim and firing their arrows or are vigorously throwing out flying balls, pursuing a frightened spotted deer. By the river, fishermen are in the process of catching fish, in the virgin forests, women and children, holding bone spades, are gathering wild fruits. As the sun goes down in the west, the village, sparkling with kitchen fires, shows women roasting meat, using stone grinders to grind meal, using bone needles to sew hemp-fabric clothes. Artists are focusing on painting or impressing patterns into ceramic vessels; old grandmothers are carefully distributing the cooked food to the others: some people are putting gathered vegetables and grains into vessels for storage.

In the northern part of the Banpo Village is the cemetery district where adults were buried. Some 174 graves have been discovered, lined up in regular order, but exhibiting different burial customs. Banpo people mostly died around the age of 30. On the eastern side of the town is the Public Kiln for firing pottery. Six kilns have been found to date. At the beginning,

Part of the Banpo residence site.

the pottery making was carried out in the open. By the time of Banpo, people had invented two main types of horizontal and upright kilns. Banpo ceramic production used both fine-grained clay and sandy coarse clay; the fine-grained was of three types depending on its use. Banpo people used realistic methods of painting to decorate their ceramics, with sketched designs to exhibit the characteristics of various animals.

Around twelve different kinds of markings or symbols have been found on pottery fragments or on vessels at the site. Together they comprise the main types of strokes used in Chinese characters, such as upright, cross-wise, hooked, and so on. Writing did not exist at the time, but these marks or symbols almost certainly contained their own meanings for people at the time. A number of daily articles are also exhibited in the museum, such as stone axes, finely made fishhooks, fish-bone forks, sharp bone needles, and all kinds of ornamentation made of stone, bone, and ivory.

Marvels of Heaven and Earth: Natural History

China's natural history museums express the common attempts of mankind to understand the world in which we find ourselves. The following describes a selection of museums that explore various aspects of our world.

Beijing Ancient Observatory

Address: Beijing City, Dongcheng District, Dongbiaobei Hutong, #2
Webite: www.bjp.org.cn

This museum looks like a turreted tower set in Beijing's ancient city walls. It is located east to the Beijing Railway Station. When it was originally built by Guo Shoujing (1231–1316) of the Yuan dynasty, it had a slightly different name but the same intent: to explore the heavens. Over the course of more than five hundred years, through Ming and Qing dynasties and on into the period after the Xinhai Revolution (1911), this location has been used to observe phenomena of the skies. This is the longest historical record of using any such observatory for so long. At present, eight large bronze implements for viewing the heavens are arrayed on the top of the museum's tower; these date from the Qing dynasty. Under the tower is a hall built between the years 1442 and 1446, during the Ming dynasty. To the east and west are subsidiary rooms and

The Beijing Ancient Observatory.

other ancient structures.

The observatory's platform, rebuilt in recent years, is 17 meters high and holds exhibition rooms inside. If you walk through the door with the three characters for the observatory carved above it, you find a three-level exhibition space devoted to China's ancient astronomical accomplishments. A stone-carved star map from Suzhou is exhibited here, as well as the ceiling astronomical map from Longfu Temple, two rare treasures. The former was done in the Song dynasty in the year 1247. It depicts 1,434 stars and is recognized as one of the best early star maps in the world. The latter was accomplished in the Ming period, but from the characters carved on

The ecliptic armillary sphere displayed on the Beijing Ancient Observatory.

the side of the map one can see that the underlying information already existed in the Tang dynasty. In the courtyard of the museum, surrounded by ancient trees, the hall and east gate areas exhibit early astronomical instruments and the methods and changes in making them. In the western chamber some 150 early methods of calculating calendars in China are exhibited. Archaic as well as more recent astronomical water clocks and contemporary astronomical clocks are exhibited. Eight bronze astronomical instruments are arranged on the top of the platform, as per the Qing-dynasty emperor Qianlong's instructions.

Part of ancient astronomic apparatus displayed on the Beijing Ancient Observatory.

Geological Museum of China

Address: Beijing, Xicheng District, Xisi, Yangrou Hutong, #15
Website: www.gmc.org.cn

The Geological Museum of China is located in Beijing at a place called Western Crossroads. It is an internationally renowned geological museum with the largest, rarest, and most valued collections in China. Its buildings cover some 11,000 square meters and contain around 200,000 items.

Begun in 1916, the museum is one of the oldest in China. In 2004, the rebuilt museum opened to the public, with an exhibition area of 4,500 square meters. It now has an earth sciences hall, an ore hall, a paleobotanical hall, a gems hall, a prehistory biological hall,

The Geological Museum of China.

A pillar-shape quartz crystal cluster of orpiment.

A trilobite fossil.

and a land and resources hall. In the prehistory biological hall, eight units cover the development of life on earth, from the earliest micro-organisms to the explosion of different life forms, to organisms becoming land creatures, to the great extinctions, to mammals and finally to hominids, or mankind.

The Museum's collections are extremely rich and contain many superlative Shantungosaurus giganteus fossils, rare fossilized primitive birds, the world's largest quartz crystal (3.5 tons), the largest mono-crystal, and so on. The earliest hominid fossil to be found to date in China is exhibited here, known as the Yuanmou-Man tooth fossil from Yunnan Province. Artefacts from Zhoukoudian, the early-hominid site outside Beijing, are also on display here.

As well as presenting material for public view, the Museum has been a research organization that carries on projects and produces publications. In this regard it has made great contributions in several areas that include dinosaur research, volcanic-activity research, work on botanical bridging of plants in the Jurassic period, and work on primitive birds in western Liaoning through fossil research that has particularly received recognition from paleobotanists around the world.

Zigong Dinosaur Museum

Address: Sichuan Province, Zigong City, Dashanpu, #238
Website: www.zdm.cn

The Zigong Dinosaur Museum is located in Dashanpu at Zigong City, on the banks of a river that flows through the western-China province of Sichuan. It is China's first museum located at the actual burial site of dinosaurs, one of three such in the world, and it covers 66,000 square meters.

"Sichuan's dinosaurs are numerous and one finds a veritable nest of them at Zigong." Zigong is a famous city for salt production, but it is also an important dinosaur fossil region in China. As a famous saying goes, one finds a veritable nest of dinosaurs at Zigong. There are more than two hundred locations within the city at which dinosaur fossils from different eras have been found. A very considerable amount of fossilized dinosaurs has been exca-

The exterior of the Zigong Dinosaur Museum.

The exhibition hall of dinosaur fossils in Zigong.

The exhibition hall that maintains the original state of excavating site of dinosaur fossils in Dashanpu, Zigong.

vated here and other vertebrate fossils have been found as well at the same sites.

The concentration of buried fossil remains at Zigong is greatest at Dashanpu. A great quantity and diversity of types is found here, including specimens that are quite rare and relatively well preserved. This place is eleven kilometers to the northeast of Zigong City. It was discovered in 1972. The fossils are in a sandy layer of the Meso-Jurassic period, from around 160,000,000 years ago. In an area of around 3,000 square meters, more than 200 individual dinosaurs have been excavated, among which more than forty are complete or relatively complete dinosaur skeletons. Especially valuable is a group of dinosaur skulls. At present, only around twenty percent of excavated dinosaurs in the world belong to the Jurassic period, and most of these are from the late Jurassic, lacking the early and middle stages that show how dinosaurs evolved. At Zigong, especially at Dashanpu, the fossils come mostly from the early and middle periods, so that this provides extremely valuable material.

The newly built Zigong Dinosaur Museum mostly exhibits fossils of dinosaurs that have been excavated from the immediate site.

The exhibition is divided into three parts:

Part 1 introduces general knowledge about fossils, botanical evolution, geologic periods, the evolution of dinosaurs and species extinctions.

Part 2 introduces the group of dinosaurs from Dashanpu. In a large space, viewers can see dinosaurs that stand 10 meters high and are 20 meters long, as well as tiny dinosaurs.

Part 3 is the actual site of dinosaur burials, in an exhibition area of 1,000 square meters. This has dinosaur bones in their original setting. Observers can look down from a railing above, but can also go down into an underground room and touch the fossils of ancient life, see the circumstances of the layers and the ores, understand the wonders and marvels of the creations of nature.

Tonglushan Ancient Metallurgy Museum

Address: Hubei Province, Huangshi City, Daye County, Tonglushan Town

Tonglushan or Tonglu Mountain is 28 kilometers from the important heavy industry town of Huangshi in Hubei Province. It is on the banks of Daye Lake which connects via waterways to the Yangtze River. Archaeologists discovered several hundred mining pits in this location and a number of copper-ore smelting furnaces that date from the early period of Western Zhou (around

The copper mining tools of the Spring and Autumn period.

The crisscross mining lanes in the Ancient Copper Mine Site.

3,000 years ago) to the Han dynasty (around 2,000 years ago), or over a period of one thousand years. Tonglushan is considered to be the cradle of ancient bronze culture in China.

In the process of extracting ore resources from under Tonglu Mountain, it was discovered that this was a large-scale refining or smelting site from ancient times. Archaeologists have to date excavated and evaluated remains from Western Zhou to Western Han periods. They have found different mining structures and support systems for several hundred wells that include vertical wells, slanted wells, blind wells and so on, as well as more than one thousand implements for mining and ore production and various implements of daily life. In addition, they discovered seventeen Song-dynasty smelting furnaces. On entering the front door of the Museum, one passes around a mammoth malachite boulder. The 1,100 square meter main hall of the site is then before one's eyes. Below the railing, looking down, one can see more than one hundred relatively well preserved vertical wells or shafts, level corridors or lanes, blind wells, slanted wells, criss-crossed mine tunnels. There are twisting channels for waterways and wooden water troughs, there are various implements of the trade spread below one's eyes. All of this makes one feel as if the workers in had just departed.

In certain places, pits and corridors have been reconstructed to allow visitors to go inside and experience for a moment the sensations of those who worked here 2,000 years ago. On walls surrounding the main hall, traditional architectural techniques have reconstructed the original posts and brackets of the Spring and Autumn Period in Chinese history.

Due to the wealth of copper ore in this location, and the long history of refining ore here, the amount of waste ore from the process is noticeable. To this day, on the surface of the ground surrounding the ore lode, there are more than 400,000 tons of ancient remains of slag. It is estimated that this site produced 8-100,000 tons of copper. The quantity of materials at the site are testimony to the outstanding technology of refining and production methods of ancient China.

Most of the ancient wells or pits that have been excavated are situated in regions that are rich in natural copper, cuprite or red copper ore, and malachite. Since the copper content of some ore taken from the wells reaches 12-20%, it can be seen that ancient craftsmen possessed the ability to read indications of promising

The exterior of the Tonglushan Ancient Metallurgy Museum.

locations. In terms of prospecting, they did shallow well testing and used washing and other methods to find high-quality ore buried beneath the surface of the earth.

In terms of extraction, under non-mechanized conditions, craftsmen used the most simple tools and materials to dig wells that were more than fifty meters deep. They created effective ways to combine vertical, slanted and blind wells with horizontal corridors; they resolved to a certain degree the problems of supporting the wells, creating air ducts, allowing for light, and expelling water. Their solutions to complex technical issues were sometimes later found in use in Europe, therefore it was once believed that some techniques had been imported. From this archaeological research it is now clear that certain structural supports and technical solutions were in use in China 2,500 years ago.

In terms of refining, the distribution of the smelting slag is extensive: the thickness of the resulting slag layer approaches three meters so that it even buries abandoned refineries that once existed here. Because of this, the slag layer preserved the surface of the land in its original state, and kept this sole example of ancient mining technology intact.

Zigong Salt History Museum

Address: Sichuan Province, Zigong City, Ziliujing District, Jiefang Road, #107

The Zigong Salt History Museum is situated in Zigong City, Sichuan Province, in buildings constructed by the salt merchants of Shaanxi. Its buildings utilize China's traditional architectural methods: an 86-meter-long central axis comprises the central hall, with the subsidiary group of buildings going up the slope of a hillside.

The picture shows the ancient salt production in China.

The exhibitions of this museum begin with an illustration from a Han-dynasty brick that was excavated in Sichuan. The illustrations on the brick depict the salt industry of the Han period and show in a lively and realistic manner the stages of salt production. Wide-mouthed shallow wells were used for early production; a two-story building and four men on the brick show how briny water was brought by conduits to heating units that cooked out the water and resulted in pure salt.

By the time of the Song dynasty, Chinese craftsmen had invented special tools for digging small-mouth-diameter wells. Not only was the mouth of the well sometimes "as small as a small bowl" but it was dug down very straight into the earth. The tools for allowing this well-tunnelling method are recorded in the "Dongpo Forest of Stelae," also exhibited at the Museum.

By the time of the transition period between Ming and Qing dynasties, the depth of these so-called Zhuotong wells reached three hundred *zhang*, a *zhang* being 3 1/3 meters, or around 1,000 meters. This museum has in its collections a relatively com-

A wood well tower in traditional salt drilling wells in Zigong.

All kinds of drilling wells and dredging tools in ancient salt wells in China.

plete set of well-digging tools, that not only could dig deeply but ensured that the well's cavity would be straight. Some modern-day well-digging technologies are a result and a continuation of this historical foundation.

Joseph Needham (1900–1995, Englishman, a world-famous historian of science and technology) listed more than twenty important inventions that had entered Europe from China in his *History of Science and Technology in China*. The fifteenth of these was the deep-well drilling technology. It is on display and well worth seeing in this unusual museum.

The exterior of the Zigong Salt Industry Historical Museum.

Appendix:
Chronological Table of the Chinese Dynasties

The Paleolithic Period	Approx. 1,700,000–10,000 years ago
The Neolithic Age	Approx. 10,000–4,000 years ago
Xia Dynasty	2070–1600 BC
Shang Dynasty	1600–1046 BC
Western Zhou Dynasty	1046–771 BC
Spring and Autumn Period	770–476 BC
Warring States Period	475–221 BC
Qin Dynasty	221–206 BC
Western Han Dynasty	206 BC–AD 25
Eastern Han Dynasty	25–220
Three Kingdoms	220–280
Western Jin Dynasty	265–317
Eastern Jin Dynasty	317–420
Northern and Southern Dynasties	420–589
Sui Dynasty	581–618
Tang Dynasty	618–907
Five Dynasties	907–960
Northern Song Dynasty	960–1127
Southern Song Dynasty	1127–1279
Yuan Dynasty	1206–1368
Ming Dynasty	1368–1644
Qing Dynasty	1616–1911
Republic of China	1912–1949
People's Republic of China	Founded in 1949